Cooking Without a Kitchen

Cooking Without a Kitchen

Marshall Berland

A & W Publishers, Inc.
NEW YORK

Copyright © 1978 by Marshall Berland

All rights reserved. No part of this work may be reproduced or transmitted in any form or by any means, electronic or mechanical, including photocopying, recording, or any information storage and retrieval system, without the permission in writing from the Publishers.

Published by
A & W Publishers, Inc.
95 Madison Avenue
New York, New York 10016

Library of Congress Catalog Card Number: 78-58764

ISBN: 0-89479-019-6
Text design by Sallie Baldwin, Antler & Baldwin, Inc.

Printed in the United States of America

To Elizabeth, who always wanted omelets.

Contents

Introduction	xiii
1. A Kitchen in a Closet	3
Appliances *11*	
Utensils *21*	
2. Game Plan for Entertaining	24
3. A Kitchen on the Go	28
The Great Getaway *29*	
Campsite Cooking *35*	
Splendor in the Grass: Picnics and Movable Feasts *38*	
The Chef At Sea *40*	
4. Getting It Together	44
The Basics *44*	
Tricks of the Trade *51*	
The Triumph of the Senses *57*	
5. Herbs and Spices	60
6. Saucery and Sorcery	72
7. Great Beginnings: Appetizers and Hors d'Oeuvres	88
8. Soups	99
9. Salads	109
10. The Egg and You	117
Eggs Cooked Plain and Simple *117*	
Variations on a Theme *118*	
Omelets *121*	
Crepes *125*	
Quiches *126*	
ENTRÉES	
11. Entrées: Barbecuing	129
12. Entrées: Beef	132

13. Entrées: Veal	153
14. Entrées: Chicken	156
15. Entrées: Ham and Pork	171
16. Entrées: Fish and Shellfish	175
17. Entrées: Pasta and Grains	188
18. Vegetables	196
19. Desserts	204
20. The Language of Cooking: A Glossary and Conversion Tables	212
Recipe Index	223

ACKNOWLEDGMENTS

I wish to thank editor Sondra Albert for her meticulous and thorough assistance as this book came to life, measured out in pinches, dashes, teaspoons, and cupsful.

I also want to thank eminent dining critic Sheldon Landwehr for his encouragement, and the owners of the fine restaurants Rive Gauche, Le Quercy, and Kaplan's at the Delmonico for their faith and continuing trust.

Introduction

I think it was Somerset Maugham who, after a long and successful career, remarked that food was the last passion to remain when the others have fled with age and that, in the final analysis, it was the truest and most satisfying one.

The pleasures of good food go far beyond eating. Few creative expressions are as immediately gratifying as the making of a memorable meal—you feel not only the appreciation of your family and friends, but the afterglow that affects the entire time spent together.

The great Russian director Konstantin Stanislavski told a group of actors that "the most fascinating thing an actor can do on stage is to fry an egg." Think of all the times you have been at a party when, as if by prearranged signal, everyone winds up in the kitchen. Whether it is done on stage, at home, or around a campfire, there is something compelling about the preparation of food—the magnetic attraction of smells, sights, and sounds bring people together.

A spacious and well-equipped kitchen is of course the ideal setting for the total enjoyment of food. One of the realities of contemporary life, however, is the fact that many of us no longer have these kitchens, either where we live or where we choose to spend our leisure time. For better or worse (and usually a little of both), cooking for today's lifestyles means learning to cook without a real kitchen.

The first thing to be sacrificed to the pressure of space and building costs seems to be the kitchen. Suburbanites often must settle for galley kitchens in tract houses. Apartment dwellers are forced to make do with "efficiency" kitchens, minimal appliances crammed into a tiny space that is anything but efficient. Some venturesome souls choose to live in places not originally meant for living—manufacturing lofts, former mills, unused country churches, even abandoned whistle-stop railroad stations—places that have no conventional kitchen facilities at all.

There are other prime candidates for *Cooking Without a Kitchen.* Many college students, living off-campus or not, want to be able to make meals in rooms not equipped for cooking. Despite all the expense-account stories we have heard, businessmen, musicians, and theater people who are on the road a great deal can ill afford the time and expense of calling room service or the boredom of eating every meal in a restaurant. Others who work in remote areas for long periods of time frequently have no access to restaurants and must provide for their own food.

On weekends, holidays, and vacations, more and more Americans take off, exchanging cramped kitchens at home for the even smaller or more primitive facilities at beach cottages and ski cabins, campers, trailers, or boat galleys. This also applies to hiking and camping trips, tailgate picnics, and country outings, where part of the fun is cooking—in this case, cooking not only without a real kitchen, but without any kitchen at all!

Accepting the culinary challenge of unorthodox environments is the first step toward a more satisfying way of life. One of the best dinners I have ever eaten—cold poached salmon, cucumber salad, white wine, and strawberries—was served picnic style on the floor of an empty apartment. It was packed into a wicker basket complete with linen, tableware, and glassware, brought by ingenious friends making this first meal in a new home a memorable one.

Cooking Without a Kitchen is dedicated to fine food and good cooking done quickly and easily without a conventional kitchen. From a simple snack to a full dinner, you can cook well and eat like a gourmet anywhere—in a tiny studio apartment or a college room, in a weekend cabin or aboard a boat. With a little imagination, you can put together an office party or a tailgate picnic for the homecoming game at your alma mater with a minimum of fuss and equipment.

Planning the recipes for this book, I have been guided by considerations of space and equipment. I apologize to those experienced cooks who may find some of the recipes too basic for them. Many cookbooks presuppose too much knowledge on the part of their readers, resulting in unnecessary confusion for the uninitiated. (One French cookbook I own actually says, "Prepare sweetbreads in the usual manner.")

One of my major objectives is to show experienced as well as beginning cooks how to prepare unusual foods without time-consuming techniques that remove the cook from the enjoyment of relaxing with families and friends.

In certain cases, classic recipes have been simplified; others have been made a bit more interesting with the addition of ingredients that add color or texture. Today when people want simple foods and natural ingredients, I think few readers will mind the occasional deletion of a calf's foot in the aspic or a cup of heavy cream in the sauce. For those who have a special interest in classic haute cuisine, there are shelves of fine cookbooks available everywhere. I have included enough variations on each basic recipe for your repertoire to be exciting, without resorting to Escoffier or *Larousse Gastronomique* and their exoticisms.

Good cooking is an art and a craft, a combination of flair and technique. No one begins as an expert; however, with a natural interest as a starting point, the rest can be cultivated and developed. If you are a novice in the kitchen, remember that just as a would-be painter must learn to draw before picking up a brush, the would-be chef must make the fundamentals before launching into a complicated feast.

Once you've learned the basics, a sense of adventure, a little ingenuity and good old-fashioned common sense will take you a long way. Cooking and eating have gone through a lot of ups and downs since man built his first fire—and most of the ups have been the result of experimentation or sheer accident. Perhaps I should have subtitled this book *Food Without Fear,* because that's just how you should approach cooking. The best philosophy I can offer for becoming a fabled cook is to enjoy what you are doing. I know that chopping onions is not a spiritual experience, but if you focus on what is to come, you'll be much better off. Very few people are known for their cooking and nothing else. Cooking is part of a general zest for living—an extension of generosity and hospitality, the logical conclusion for experimental souls.

One essential ingredient is a sense of humor. Once, during one of her television performances, Julia Child dropped a suckling pig on the floor. Unflustered, she smiled into the camera, picked up the piglet, replaced it on the platter, and went right on trimming it with sprigs of parsley. "Remember," she said, "you're alone in the kitchen!" Very sage advice. Few people will fault you for an overcooked vegetable when there is animated conversation and genuine conviviality. If you keep this in mind, the odds for a super dinner are definitely in your favor.

Everyone is different, so you'll have to learn from your own experience when to experiment with new dishes and when you'll feel more comfortable sticking to your existing repertoire of tried-and-true recipes. I have always found that when I am giving a really important dinner I'd rather make something that I've made before. Preparing what you know is good makes for a more relaxed meal, and usually a better one. Another bit of advice, especially if you are having more than a few guests, is to keep to dishes that do not have a tricky timetable. In the first place, you'll want to spend time with them rather than be stuck in the kitchen. Furthermore, the meal will flow more smoothly if you can keep serving time elastic.

Naturally, we all know those miraculous, infuriating souls who can turn a can of sardines, some crackers, and a head of limp lettuce into a banquet. (We also know others who will follow an elaborate recipe to the letter, in a fully equipped kitchen, and still fail.)

Cooking Without a Kitchen aims somewhere between these extremes, with explained guidelines and basic techniques to be used at home or away on holiday. It is for people who want to accomplish a few minor miracles without the aid of a complete kitchen or a diploma from the Cordon Bleu cooking school. Believe me, with a little practice, you'll make it!

Cooking Without a Kitchen

1
A Kitchen in a Closet

Where there's a whim, there's a way. Once you open your mind to the possibility of improvising a cooking area where none exists, the fun begins.

Not so long ago, conventional houses and apartments were considered the only places to live. With the relaxation of rigid social conventions and the resurgence of individualism, more and more people all over the country are exploring novel ways to make the places where they live (and sometimes work as well) better suited to individual needs and preferences. It's all part of a revival of the frontier spirit of our beginnings, a return to essential priorities. One of the pulses of today's freer lifestyles is the option to choose life in unstructured living spaces, never intended for living at all.

New York's SoHo district and Chicago's Old Town are only two examples of the changing character of inner city living, as well as the changing face of the inner city itself. Decaying manufacturing and warehouse areas are becoming vital, living neighborhoods. Exciting developments such as these are taking place all over the country, in suburban and rural areas as well as in cities. Adventurous people are accepting the challenge of abandoned mills and canneries, carriage houses and stables, barns, village churches, and deserted railway stations. Such interesting landmarks are being preserved and converted into viable living spaces, despite the lack of those conventional kitchen "necessities" that were once considered of primary importance.

The range of solutions is enormous when you start to create cooking facilities where none previously existed. I once visited an elaborate estate in the hills above Cannes on the French Riviera.

Its mistress, a wealthy divorcée from Philadelphia noted for her lavish hospitality, lives alone in a sixteenth-century priory, converting the rambling buildings into a remarkable villa complete with all the most modern American plumbing and kitchen facilities. One building was refurbished as a two bedroom guesthouse, with a maid's room upstairs, to attend to the needs of her guests. The main house, with thick stone walls, became her residence, with the dining room downstairs; an ancient potting shed became the cook's domain, with a connecting passageway between them fitted out as a butler's pantry. Fresh flowers from immaculately tended gardens were everywhere, replaced at the first sign of a wilted petal by an army of maids. In all, the house represents one of the last survivors of a lifestyle now virtually unknown anywhere.

Of course, the combination of imagination and money can make anything possible, but few of us have the kind of financial resources necessary to create and maintain such an establishment. A more realistic example is that of a neighbor of mine in the country, an artist who moved from a small Greenwich Village apartment to an unused firehouse in upstate New York. The building, with great high windows and large uninterrupted spaces, was perfectly suited to her work and lifestyle. Since the down payment took most of her savings (as would be the case with most of us), major renovations, like installing the perfect kitchen, would have to be done in stages later on. In the meantine, she did remarkably well on ingenuity alone. Fortunately, an old sink and decrepit refrigerator happened to be there already. For cooking, she organized a combination of portable electrical appliances, choosing them with an eye for what would be useful when she would be able to put in a "real" kitchen. With a toaster-oven and a double hot plate, plus an inexpensive hibachi charcoal grill for barbecuing outdoors, she turned out delicious, inventive meals—with her artist's eye for combining foods with interesting colors and textures.

Between these two extremes—the one permanent and expensive, the other temporary and economical—there is a vast range of possibilities. Before you rush ahead, though, stop and consider some pertinent questions so you can come up with the best solution for your own particular situation and needs.

To begin with, how often do you want to cook, and how much? This may seem obvious, but your answer is basic to everything that follows. If all you may need or want is a sandwich or eggs and coffee in the morning, it's ridiculous to set up a battery of appliances and tableware, pots and pans. If you are not sure, start small; you can always expand as you get into it. For sandwiches and coffee, get (or borrow) a few plates and cups, some flatware from the local five and dime, and maybe a few place mats, if you feel elegant. An immersion coil will heat water in your cup for coffee, tea, or instant soup. (There are also cheap aluminum coffeepots you can get anywhere.) Eggs can be cooked in a small pot or skillet on a hot plate. That's about as minimal as you can get and still call it cooking. But for a midnight snack or breakfast—particularly when you are traveling or in another short-term situation—it can be sufficient.

On the other hand, whatever you set up should be able to do more than make coffee and eggs. With the increasing costs of a college education, more and more students want to cook in their rooms, if for no other reasons than convenience and simple economics. Times may change, but I'm sure things are not all that different now than my college days. When I was at the University of Wisconsin, hunger pangs always struck just as the last "greasy spoon" on campus closed for the night. Out of utter desperation, I created a mini-kitchen in my room which could be stored out of sight when not in use—and hidden from the prying eyes of the landlady! It consisted of an electric frying pan, a percolator, and a hot plate, with a couple of small pans. I kept small quantities of a few staples in a box under the bed and bought fresh foods as I used them. It may not have been The Four Seasons or Maxim's, but I survived those all-night study sessions before exams and even managed a few meals for friends.

Dancers and actors proverbially bring some kind of cooking utensils when they go on the road. Their notoriously low salaries and off-beat working hours make it a matter of survival. (Remember *Gypsy?*) Even if they don't need it for survival, it can be a good idea for other travelers, businessmen, real estate agents, country attorneys, and those whose work keeps them in remote areas away from decent restaurants, or who are just too busy to take the time to eat out.

Carrying your kitchen with you can be a real economy for vacationers. A few years ago, I spent my vacation in a small cottage (euphemistically called a villa by the real estate agent) in Montego Bay, Jamaica. There were three of us, and after a short conference we decided to do breakfast and lunch at the cottage, saving our money for fancy dinners in good restaurants. The cottage had a small refrigerator and we picked up a cheap toaster-oven and a double hot plate in town. The cottage had a few dishes, two pots, and a frying pan. We made out beautifully—shopping for food in the native markets was great fun, one of the best ways to get to know the people of a place.

Making a few breakfasts, lunches, and an occasional dinner in these temporary situations can be fun—almost a game—and an extra facet of the overall enjoyment. Cooking regularly with inadequate or nonexistent facilities, however, is a whole different ball game. The satisfaction of creating a workable kitchen from unpromising beginnings, making pleasant meals day after day, and serving creative dinners—this is an accomplishment of a completely different magnitude. I've done it, and it is worth the effort.

Actually, it just takes a bit of logic and planning. After all, what is a kitchen, anyway? Picture the fanciest kitchen you have ever seen in the pages of *House and Garden*. What did it actually contain?—one or more sinks and stoves, a refrigerator, dishwasher, garbage disposal (perhaps now a compactor), acres of counter space, and storage cabinets. Fine to work in, of course, but how much is absolutely necessary? Think about it. However nice and convenient these things are, a sink, refrigerator, stove, and a usable working and storage area are all that are really essential. You may not even have these basics in your living space, but if you overcome the idea that a kitchen must have all these things (and have them all in one place), you are on your way to a solution. Take a look at these things one by one and see how the difficulties can be overcome with a little improvisation.

For those who want to create a reasonable facsimile of a kitchen, or to augment what they have, the first question is: Do you have a sink or running water? Either you do or you don't. But don't despair. Naturally, a good big sink is preferable, but as long as you have access to water, you can rig up a workable water supply for cooking. It may be a little bizarre, but it will work. Buy a five-gallon (or larger) plastic container with a spigot at the bottom like a picnic thermos. These are available at camping outfitters or chemical supply houses (some of which cater to mail-order customers). If you're really determined, with a little hunting you should be able to find one. If you place the container on a shelf with the spigot at a convenient height for your cooking and washing needs, a plastic dishpan can be placed underneath the spigot to catch the water. If you simply can't find a container with a spigot, a large watering can is clumsier but it can do the job.

The galley kitchen of my New York apartment, whose inadequacy originally prompted this book, has a sink with approximately the same dimensions as a sheet of typing paper—just about big enough for rinsing an olive. It was easier to wash dishes in a plastic dishpan filled from the tub, rinse them in the sink, and place them in a dish rack to drain. If worse comes to worst, and you don't have a sink near your cooking area, you can carry washed dishes in the dishpan and rinse them in your bathroom. I know it is inconvenient and a bit grungy, but it can be the easiest way to tackle the problem.

Is there a refrigerator available? If necessary, you can make a meal without refrigeration, but if you can find the space and afford the expense, I think you'll find that a refrigerator is a worthwhile investment. Refrigerators come in a variety of sizes and price ranges, in all sorts of colors and finishes, and with any number of optional gadgets and special features. Frost-free models, for example, will save you the time and mess of defrosting; but they are more expensive to buy and use significantly more electricity than do standard models (in addition to the cost, this is a point to remember if you're interested in conserving energy).

I have never heard anyone complain about a refrigerator being too big, so naturally, a full-size unit with a spacious freezer compartment is to be desired. If space is at a premium, consider one of the small under-the-counter refrigerators used in studio apartments, or an even smaller office-size model. Some are made with a wood-grain finish to make them look more like furniture. This is something to keep in mind if you are going to keep your refrigerator in an unlikely place—a little wood-grained office model could take the place of an end table next to your sofa.

You don't have to buy a new refrigerator. If money is tight, you can usually pick up a serviceable used one from a local appliance dealer. Of course, remember that buying a used appliance is like buying a used car. It's a case of "buyer beware." Still, if you poke around a bit and buy from a reputable merchant, a used refrigerator can be a good buy.

Money spent on a refrigerator is seldom wasted. If you move to larger quarters, you can always use it in a family room or office, or as a standby when you are giving a big party.

If you don't want the expense of buying a major appliance, however, and have easy access to a grocery or supermarket, you can do without a refrigerator. Buy your perishables as you need them. You can keep them in an ice-filled picnic cooler. Camping outfitters, and some department and hardware stores, sell metal picnic chests, but the "igloo" plastic foam coolers carried by supermarkets and five-and-dime stores are just as good or even better, and considerably cheaper. A word of advice: The tiny spaces in the walls of molded Styrofoam coolers tend to trap mildew, so it is a good idea to wash them out with a disinfectant periodically, and always let them air-dry unclosed.

Where water supply and refrigeration are concerned, ad-libbing a kitchen in a closet or a corner is pretty straightforward. The last (actually, it's probably the first) basic element of any kitchen, however makeshift, is heat, and here you really have a lot of options. Many foods can be served without being cooked—and I've included as many of these recipes as possible. If you're serious about cooking, though, and mean to do it with any degree of regularity, you must have something on which or in which to cook (or heat) your food. Naturally a stove is the best general appliance for cooking. But unlike a refrigerator, which is simply plugged into a wall outlet, stoves may require the installation of gas or special power lines. Like water, if it's not there already, you'll have to forget about the stove—unless the kitchen you're contemplating is to be a permanent addition and worth the expense. In the meantime, you can get along very nicely without a stove. There are dozens of portable electric appliances (and probably hundreds of combination cooking vessels and appliances). With these, you can boil and broil, sauté and stew, bake and grill, toast and roast, steep and brew. Most of them are within the average budget (unless you buy one of each!). Before you grab your checkbook and dash out to the nearest department store, think about what you are likely to do fairly regularly. Then read the following section on appliances. Begin by selecting what will give you the greatest range of functions for your own needs. Starting small is the best way to avoid wasting money. Also consider what will remain useful if you ever change your living quarters, or modernize your weekend retreat with a real kitchen. Will what you buy now add to your enjoyment of cooking?

The Appliance Checklist may be equally useful for those of you who do have a stove in your efficiency kitchen. The basic appliances usually provided in these two-by-four so-called kitchens can always be augmented by well-selected portable cooking aids.

A few words of caution about using electric appliances. Make absolutely certain that your electric wiring is adequate for what you plan to do. Heat-producing appliances—toasters, broilers, and frying pans—utilize what is called resistance heat and use a great deal of power. To keep from overloading the circuits, never operate more than one such appliance at a time from the same power source. Whenever possible, plug the appliance directly into a wall outlet. If you must use an extension cord, be sure it is a heavy-duty one that will not overheat when used with appliances, and that it has a three-pronged grounded plug for additional safety from shock. Never leave your cooking area unattended. If you are careless, at the very least you run the risk of blowing a fuse; you may also start a potentially tragic fire. This isn't intended to frighten you—just to remind you of the old adage about an ounce of prevention being worth a pound of cure. Almost any appliance you buy today can be used safely, as long as it is used properly. Enough said!

Again, remembering college days when I had one room with a small sink, I set up the cooking utensils on a drop-leaf table, with pots and pans in a carboard box inside the closet. (There was the added adventure of an inquisitive landlady sniffing for telltale odors of forbidden cooking in the rooms, so that these forays in cooking took on a quality of foreign intrigue that I'm sure enhanced the meals.)

Beyond these hardship conditions, if there is a refrigerator and some place to wash vegetables and dishes, it is possible to do almost anything. If you have a little empty wall space or a closet (or both), you can arrange a group of shelves, using any one of several adjustable systems that are now available in department and variety stores. (If you are securing these to hollow walls, be sure to use molly or toggle bolts made especially for this purpose.) Shelves should be from 10 inches to a foot deep, to accommodate pots and pans.

For actual cooking, use shelves or a table in the room itself, if at all possible. If you want to disguise the kitchen, you can close off the shelves with a curtain or shutters. If you need to use a closet, though, use the door. An old-fashioned solid wood door is ideal, since the newer ones are hollow and will not support as much weight. For maximum efficiency, put up a drop-leaf shelf, 12 to 14 inches deep, at waist height for serving. You can find the hinges and other materials in a hardware store. Above this, use pegboard, held away from the surface by wood lath strips at least one-quarter inch thick, so you can insert hooks to hold your cooking materials. (Be sure to allow for clearance when the closet door is closed or you'll end up like the man who built his sailboat in his basement, only to find that he couldn't get it out.) Average closet doors range from 28 inches to around 34 inches across, and judicious planning can make room for an astonishing array of materials.

Since space is at a premium, organize it (and add a decorative touch as well) by outlining the location of each utensil or appliance with paint or a Magic Marker—ensuring its return to the proper place. Kitchen tools and flatware can be stored in empty coffee cans hung on hooks. Large-size empty juice cans will hold spatulas and longer tools like wooden spoons. These cans can be covered with decorative Contact plastic if you wish.

Again, it is strongly advised that you use this closet arrangement for storage and serving only—using a table or counter for actual preparation—because of the obvious safety hazard of using heat and electrical appliances in a precarious position. (And also to avoid having your clothes smell like last night's dinner!) Preparation space, if possible, should have a hard durable surface that can be easily cleaned. Formica and other scratch-resistant surfaces are ideal, and with some practice can be installed by you or a handy friend. If this is not possible, be sure to get a large enough chopping block and metal-covered asbestos pads for your appliances. Start your cooking with breakfast, and in no time at all, you'll be cooking full meals with the best of them.

Appliances

What kind of appliances should you get? Today the sky's the limit. A trip through the small-appliances department of your local store will set your head reeling with the possibilities. After inspecting the price tags and considering your budget, you'll be able to establish a realistic order of priorities—what you need and what you can live without.

What kind of cooking will you want to do, and for how many? Considering your personal living arrangements and food preferences, how often will you be using a particular appliance, and is there room for it? You'll be able to decide very easily whether you can live without an electric can opener or juice extractor, and it will keep you from having a boxful of abandoned materials if you change your lifestyle.

Happily, there are a whole range of new affordable appliances with more than one function. Toaster-ovens can broil and bake as well as make toast; some electric frying pans and crock pots can double as ovens. If you are trying to economize, remember that sometimes spending a few extra dollars on a single appliance can eliminate the need for buying two separate ones.

If you are unfamiliar with a new appliance or manufacturer, check one of the consumer reports or a reliable merchant to get the real story. Also, don't try to save money by purchasing something that will be too small for your needs. These economies can turn out to be a real waste. When presented with a choice, opt for the larger size. (Like buying clothes for a growing child, you will quickly be needing the extra room—for parties, unexpected guests, that occasional larger-than-usual roast or stew.)

The quality of an appliance—how well it is made and will do the job—is something else you must consider. Whatever it is, try to get a brand that you are familiar with, and be sure it has a UL (Underwriters Laboratory) seal of approval. This will mean that it has been tested and is safe for normal use. Sometimes, an off brand can prove unsatisfactory after a short time and you have no recourse to the manufacturer. Be sure to look for some kind of guarantee or warranty.

On the other hand, you might as well try to get the best price, so shop in discount stores. This is not really a contradiction in terms. The warranty is given by the manufacturer, not the retailer, and if an appliance breaks down, it usually must be returned to the manufacturer. A reputable retailer, even a discount store, should be willing to exchange a new appliance if it is faulty—but you should ask about the store's policy beforehand.

After buying the necessities, if there is something else you really want, get it. Each of us has his own eccentricities. (Mine is a new automatic coffee machine. I use it for daily coffee, brewing tea, making instant soups, anything that needs boiling water.) Your hang-up may be an electric ice cream machine, a doughnut fryer, or something else. Indulge yourself. After all, it's your money.

The following suggestions should help you make up your mind about what to get. Most, though not all, are electrical. They are described by type rather than by function, since many of them have several uses.

ELECTRIC FRYING PANS

These versatile cooking appliances seem to be able to do everything but whistle "Dixie." For openers, they can, of course, fry and sauté everything from meats to omelets, slowly simmer vegetables or a stew at an even temperature, "French fry" potatoes and shellfish. Certain models can be used for baking (on a wire rack). Look for a model with thermostatic controls in a removable handle, so the pan can be totally immersed in water for easy washing. Also, try to get one with a Teflon or similar nonstick coating inside. (The earlier models with an inner coating would scratch easily, but newer ones seem to be more durable. Nonetheless, it is advisable to use a nylon or wooden spatula or spoon in cooking just to be on the safe side. This applies to all coated appliances, of course.) Some have glass covers, which make it easier to check on what's cooking, but a high-domed metal cover with a vent that can be opened to allow steam to escape is more practical. This one appliance can become the nucleus of your cooking center, and luckily, they are not very expensive.

TOASTER-BROILERS

Except for cooking liquids, these perform most of the other cooking functions that are not possible in the electric frying pan. They are a good investment, and virtually dozens of sizes and models are available in a wide range of prices. Naturally, the simplest toaster-broiler is the cheapest. Prices climb as additional functions multiply. At the very least, you should choose one with both an upper and a lower coil and an adjustable tray. For years, I used a simple nonautomatic broiler like this. It was fine for making toast and open-faced grilled sandwiches as well as for broiling steaks and hamburgers, fish and bacon. You can also use the top as a warmer for other foods prepared in advance.

Some models have a thermostat with actual temperature settings, others have graduated settings which, with a little experience, are very easy to use. Try to look for one with a glass door to keep smoke and cooking fats from escaping. More expensive models can have an automatic timer, and some of the larger models have a motorized rotisserie with a revolving spit for broiling fowl and meats. If you have the cash and the room, these are well worth it, since as the food revolves, it bastes itself, with excess fats dropping into the pan below. (You can also stop the motor periodically and add barbecuing sauces.)

If you don't feel the need for all these functions, buy a conventional toaster, but the difference in cost between them is not great enough to offset the convenience of these multifunctional appliances.

TOASTER-OVENS

These are quite compact, if space is a major concern, and new models have a broiler feature as well as toasting and baking capabilities. For the single person or a couple, they are fine for baking a couple of potatoes or a little loaf cake, half a chicken or a small steak, but they are really too small for general cooking needs.

HOT PLATES

If you really don't need or can't afford an electric frying pan or broiler, you can get by with a double hot plate, either the ones with an electric coil in a ceramic shell or the newer models with a solid heating surface. Again, these are available almost everywhere, and are inexpensive and easy to use. The cheaper ones have two heat settings (low and high) and better models have graduated controls with more flexibility. Although I personally

A KITCHEN IN A CLOSET 15

don't like them—if you are not careful, foods can scorch easily—you can get along with one of these and a couple of pots and pans as a start.

COFFEE MAKERS

An entire chapter could be devoted to coffee makers. Suffice it to say that what you should get is strictly a matter of personal preference and budget. With your hot plate, you can make good coffee in a glass Chemex or Melitta drip-method coffee maker, boiling the water in an ordinary pan and pouring it through the coffee held in a paper filter. Electric percolators are not expensive and come in a variety of sizes and price ranges. The new automatic drip machines can also be used to keep the coffee or tea hot without having to remove the grounds, as one has to do with some percolators, which start perking again periodically if left on for a while. And of course, many people swear by the magical powers of their favorite old percolator or dripolator, which require an outside heat source such as a hot plate or stove.

ELECTRIC FOOD WARMERS

These keep foods at serving temperature without drying out, which can be vital if you are trying to prepare a full meal with a limited number of cooking sources. Made by a number of manufacturers, they are available in a wide variety of shapes, sizes, and prices.

ELECTRIC SLOW COOKERS (OR CROCK POTS)

This appliance is becoming increasingly popular since its introduction a few years ago. The basic principle is a modern adaptation of the old bean pot, in which foods are cooked very slowly with gentle heat for a long time. The cooking temperature is usually around 185 degrees—high enough to cook but too low to boil or break down most vegetable fibers. They are quite versatile and some can be adapted to bake certain breads and cakes. But they are also geared to people who have 5 to 10 hours lead time for cooking a meal, and who are sufficiently organized to have everything ready to go into the pot when they begin their day. (Theoretically, the meal that starts cooking at 8:00 A.M. will be ready for serving at 6:00 P.M.) Costs vary widely among the many units available, depending on size and manufacturer. There is now a metal version, large enough for roasting a chicken. The base, which has the heating element, can be separated and also used as a griddle. I recently bought a 3½-quart-capacity stoneware model with a glass top. Now that I have experimented with this kind of cooking for a while, I wish that I had purchased the larger 5-quart model with a removable crock, which can be immersed in water and is less awkward to wash. However, since the cooking temperature never gets very high, it is not quite as bad as scrubbing burnt food from a conventional pot.

There is a special way of cooking in these appliances, which I suppose one can get used to. Since not much heat is involved, overcooking seldom results. In addition, because the heat is slow and even, liquids do not boil off, and you must allow for this. I found, for example, that my favorite French beef stew recipe, made in a crock pot according to the manufacturer's directions, was tender, but the sauce was a bit watery and lacked its usual gusto, even after I cooked it uncovered for a while at the high setting, as the directions suggested. Chili made in a slow cooker is very good, and soups are excellent.

Once more, it is up to you to determine whether this is an appliance that will be used enough to justify its purchase. Make your own choice, but if you do get one, take my advice and select one of the larger models with a pot that can be immersed in water for washing. Since there are quite a number of cookbooks devoted exclusively to the subject of crockery cookery, I have not covered it extensively. In general, anything that should be simmered slowly, such as a soup or stew, can be made successfully in a slow stoneware cooker, following the manufacturer's directions about amounts of liquid and cooking time.

PRESSURE COOKERS

There are as many fads in appliances as there are in anything else. When I was growing up, pressure cookers were the rage, and there were endless versions of the story of what happened when the pot blew up, spattering food all over the kitchen ceiling. Improvements have been made and safety features built into newer versions, however, and the basic principle of using steam pressure to cook food very quickly is a sound one. Where crockery cookers take hours, pressure cookers take only minutes. They can be tricky, since a minute more or less can make a great deal of difference. Timing is essential, and if you are a casual cook, they probably are not for you. Nevertheless, pressure cooking is one of the best ways to steam fresh vegetables; since very little water is used and cooking is so rapid, they retain more of their food value than in conventional cooking, where most of the vitamins and other nutrients are poured off with the cooking water. As long as the meat is browned first, in less than a half hour you can also make a quite respectable stew that would ordinarily take three to four hours.

ELECTRIC WOKS

Another of today's very popular appliances, this is simply a modern electrified version of the classic age-old Chinese cooking pot. Essentially a round-bottomed frying pan with gently sloping sides, the wok is used for the entire vocabulary of Oriental stir-fried foods. This very wholesome method of cooking uses small pieces of meat, fowl, or fish combined with uniformly cut pieces of vegetables, which are quite literally "stir-fried"—chased around the sloping sides of the wok with a special spatula as they cook. Cooking itself is very quick; the real time is spent in preparation, dicing, and slicing the ingredients with an ultrasharp cleaver or knife. I'm very enthusiastic about wok cookery. It is a delicious, beautiful, and wholesome method of preparing food, with crispy, crunchy vegetables in velvety sauces. Far from being difficult and exotic, it is actually very easy to master.

If you have a conventional gas stove, you may want to consider a traditonal stove-top wok. These are now available in many places and are considerably less expensive and more compact than the electric versions. You can try some of the Chinese and Japanese recipes included here even without a wok—just use a skillet or frying pan with a large enough surface to cook everything at the same temperature and at the same time. There is an additional feeling of accomplishment to be gained in the mastery (or at least the attempt) of some of the world's finest cuisine.

MICROWAVE OVENS

These alluring space-age ovens have captured the imagination (and the dollars) of more and more people since their relatively recent introduction, despite the unresolved question of their safety. They range from expensive to very expensive, and from reasonably simple to veritable computer centers that combine the principles of conventional and microwave cooking and can change heat, brown, defrost, and bake. I have used them only occasionally, I admit, but my initial reaction is that they are fine for anyone who lives primarily on frozen foods, needs to defrost them quickly, and doesn't mind the "steam-table" quality of the results. I realize that I will be descended on by hordes of believers, but since my subject is cooking *without* a kitchen, I will leave these bulky, expensive appliances to be dealt with by specialized cookbooks.

ELECTRIC FRENCH FRYERS

Once more, I claim a personal prejudice. In today's world, where we are more and more aware of how food affects health (and especially of the potential dangers of cholesterol and saturated fats), I feel that the inclusion of these deep-frying appliances in a limited kitchen is an unnecessary expense, if not to say a health hazard. (The manufacturer of one deep fat fryer on the market even suggests that you keep reusing the fat for successive fryings! The very idea makes the mind boggle. If you don't believe me, ask your doctor.) True, there is something sinfully delicious about deep fat-fried foods, but if these are part of your own cooking repertoire, you can always use your regular electric frying pan.

BLENDERS

This is another one of those appliances you won't know you've missed until you have one. Blenders are very handy for puréeing, chopping, and homogenizing. (Such foods as mayonnaise and hollandaise sauces require a blender—or an arm like a baseball pitcher). They can also chop ice, mix drinks, and perform many other useful functions. Some models even have heating elements, so they can cook as they blend—a good idea if you are making creamy soups and sauces. There are also battery-operated blenders for outdoor and camping use.

ELECTRIC MIXERS

These do some of the things that blenders cannot, such as whip cream, mix bread or cake batter, and combine anything to a uniform consistency without chopping it into very fine pieces. A small electric hand mixer is inexpensive and can be kept in a drawer when not in use. You won't die without it, but it can come in handy. Battery-operated as well as plug-in models are available, although for cooking away from home, you might as well use a wire whisk.

Once you pick out the appliances you really need for basic cooking, you may want to consider some of the frills. You alone will know whether owning any of them will make your life complete, so my advice is: Turn on whatever turns you on!

Waffle irons come in various sizes and shapes. Some of the newer models also have flip-over grills that can be used for hamburgers and grilled sandwiches.

Electric coffee grinders are the last word for the coffee addict. If you are one of those people who make coffee a ritual, these little mills allow you to make freshly ground coffee as you need it, from coarse to the fine grind used for espresso, Turkish, and Greek coffee.

Electric knives make child's play out of carving fowl and

roasts. Either battery-operated or plug-in, they can be very useful when entertaining.

Electric can openers. In this age of electronics, even the lowly can of pork and beans gets special treatment. If much of your diet comes out of cans, you might want one. (Frankly, I'd save my money for something that contributed more significantly to my well-being.)

Electric juicers and juice extractors. These are not the same thing. The first is a reamer which looks like any ordinary orange-juice squeezer except it is electric, with a perforated base to separate the juice from the pulp and seeds. They are often available as optional attachments to electric mixers. Juice extractors are much fancier (and costlier) gadgets for the health-food set. They break down fruits and vegetables into juice and fibers. People who own these expensive machines say they are worth it. If you are into carrot-, celery-, or beet-juice cocktails, this is right for you.

Electric and manual food mills. These machines grind raw and cooked meat, and almost anything else, to a pulp. Again, only you can tell how much this means to you.

Just to show you how far our civilization has progressed, with a minimum of effort you can also get your own hot dog cooker, peanut butter machine, yogurt maker, electric popcorn popper, egg poacher, ice cream machine. (This one, I must admit, has always tempted me, but so far I have resisted.) A whole paradise of electrical gadgetry appears in the various holiday catalogs from better department stores and direct-mail collections. Hammacher Schlemmer in New York caters to almost any whim—as long as you can afford the tab. For those fortunate souls in the Rolls-Royce league, there are several new food processing machines available that seem to perform every possible function but actually eat the food. Cuisinart and La Machine are imported from France and others are made by major U.S. companies. All are expensive, but they will chop vegetables and grind raw meat, purée, make dough, whip, homogenize, shred, whatever. They could do away

A KITCHEN IN A CLOSET   21

with all the separate individual utensils for the kitchen. (Even if you decide not to get one, it is fun to look at what they can do.)

Utensils

There is an old saying that it is a poor workman who blames his tools. Needless to say, some people get the bends when they don't have the security of a fully equipped kitchen. But if you have your act together, you can manage magnificently with surprisingly few basic tools. For each person, these basics will be different. With apologies to Julie Andrews, these are a few of *my* favorite things:

A cleaver. This can double as a utility knife, meat pounder, vegetable slicer and dicer, cheese cutter, etc. In Oriental cooking, the cleaver is used for almost all cutting and chopping. Get one with a large heavy blade to slice through raw meat and cut fowl apart at the joint. The authentic Oriental ones rust almost instantly, so if you don't want to oil it every time you use it, get a cleaver with a stainless steel blade.

A pepper mill. In my eyes, this is an essential. The fragrant addition of freshly ground pepper (not the preground stuff) can add that indefinable something to a dish. Get used to grinding your own pepper as you need it—it's one of the hallmarks of a good cook.

From fish poachers to egg coddlers, the number of cooking vessels, kitchen gadgets, and instruments you can buy is limitless. For a workable kitchen in a closet, the following (in addition to the essential cleaver and pepper mill) should be more than adequate:

A 6- to 8-quart pot with a tight-fitting cover, or a Dutch oven (preferably baked enamel on cast iron) for spaghetti, stews, soups, even as an emergency dishpan.

A 9-inch skillet or omelet pan with a cover.

22 Cooking Without a Kitchen

A set of graduated saucepans, with covers. For rice, vegetables, sauces, etc.

A broiling pan with a wire rack, or a deeper roasting pan with a rack and cover. (If you have room, it's good to have both.)

A vegetable steamer. An inexpensive gadget that is placed inside a tightly covered saucepan. The best way to cook vegetables.

A good coffeepot—percolator or drip. Use for boiling water as well as for coffee. Consider buying an electric coffee maker.

A large plastic pitcher with screw-on lid and closable pouring spout. For juices, iced tea, etc.

A colander or large strainer. For draining and rinsing everything from salads to spaghetti.

A cutting board or chopping block. It can double as a platter for serving barbecued meats and fish.

An old-fashioned 4-sided metal grater.

A potato peeler—the kitchen's "Little Giant."

A set of very sharp kitchen knives (butcher knife, paring knife, and steak knives).

Poultry shears. A pair of heavy kitchen scissors handy for cutting up fowl, trimming fins, and any number of other chores.

A garlic press. The extra-large size also can be used for squeezing lemons, onions, or anything juicy.

A basting syringe. (You'll use it more often than you think!)

A set of measuring spoons and a 2-cup measuring cup.

Wooden spoons. Get several different sizes. If you have good pots, wooden spoons will help avoid scratches.

A rubber or plastic spatula.

A pancake turner.

Kitchen tongs. For spaghetti, fried chicken, anything that needs attention while being cooked.

Pot holders or heatproof oven mitts (with long cuffs for barbecuing).

Large serving spoon and fork. Toss salad with them as well.

Closable salt and pepper shakers. Where it is humid, put raw rice in salt.

A KITCHEN IN A CLOSET   23

A bottle opener, a good corkscrew, and a can opener. The combination instrument invariably will chew up the cork on a wine bottle.

A dish drainer and mat.

A plastic dishpan or pail.

Sponges, steel wool pads, or a pot scrubbing brush, and dish washing soap.

A garbage pail and plastic trash bags.

Aluminum foil and plastic wrap (or resealable bags).

Paper towels. For wiping and drying, of course, but you can also use them as emergency coffee filters.

2
Game Plan for Entertaining

These days an adequate kitchen is as rare as an income-tax cut. Entertaining under these conditions requires the timing of a Rockette and the steely nerves of General Patton.

Here are a few basics you might consider before launching your party which can keep at least some of your anxieties under control:

- For any party—and especially if you are serving food, be it a sit-down dinner or a buffet supper—RSVP's should be requested to make life bearable. It is perfectly proper to invite people by phone, but try to pin them down.

- Naturally, you can expect late comers, but if your party is during the week and suburbanites are expected, consider starting early enough for them to get the last train to Scarsdale without feeling that they missed all the fun.

- Unless you are planning a loosely structured open house with drinks, keep the cocktail hour to just that. If the food arrives much later, chances are you will have to cope with a guest or two who has had a little too much to drink, which just makes it harder for you. (Even if it is to be just drinks, there should be something to nibble on, especially during the holidays, since some of your guests will probably be going on to other parties and they'll appreciate the sustenance.) An easy and very attractive hors d'oeuvre is what the French call crudités—bite-size chunks of almost any firm, colorful vegetable, which can include the usual salad fixings as well as some you might not think of eating raw, for example: broccoli, cauliflower, summer squash, and zucchini—served with a creamy blue cheese dressing for dipping (see page 77). They will also appeal to guests who are watching their weight.

- If your budget permits, champagne should be considered as the sole drink. It has the advantage of being the one beverage that can properly be served from cocktails all the way through dinner to the dessert, and the cost will not differ greatly between a respectable French nonvintage Champagne or a less expensive domestic brand and the variety of liquors and mixes that you would have to buy. If possible, try to serve champagne in tulip-shaped glasses or the tall slender flutes that look like a miniature pilsner glass. These make the most of the bubbles—the flat coupe shape so often used in this country really does not do justice to the wine.

- If there are more people than you can comfortably manage at table, opt for a buffet with a substantial main dish—a stew or casserole with meat and vegetables—with a mixed green salad and wine or cold beer. (The new crock pots can be brought out to keep the main dish hot until you are ready to serve.) Chili has become one of the new standard fares for entertaining, and with good reason. There are about three hundred absolutely "authentic" recipes around, and if this is your choice, you can rest assured that most of your guests will love it. See page 139.

Although it sounds like sacrilege, I sometimes send for the premixed spices made under the colorful brand name of Wick Fowler's 2-Alarm Chili. They aren't kidding about the 2-alarm part—it is hotter than hell, used full strength, and I usually use only half of the red pepper supplied, or make a double recipe with the ingredients supplied. It is available here and there in gourmet shops. You can write for information to: Caliente Chili, Inc., P.O. Drawer 5340, Austin, Texas 78763. They will tell you where to find it in your area and how to order by mail.

- This brings up a crucial point: Don't gamble with your guests. Although that recipe in last Sunday's *New York Times* or the *Daily Bugle* looks irresistible, make something that you know will work well—the uncertainty of trying a new culinary tour de force for a party just isn't worth the trouble.

- You know your friends. If you think they would enjoy it, the classically simple wine and cheese party can be the ideal way to entertain without any cooking at all. (This is especially good for an office party, or when there is really no time to prepare for guests after working all day.) There is a wide selection of distinctive domestic wines available in attractive jugs just about everywhere at reasonable prices, and most places will have a selection of bulk white wines already cooled. Select a number of different cheeses, figuring on a minimum of a quarter of a pound per person. Depending on what is available locally, you should choose a variety of different tastes and textures from the following:

    Soft ripening cheeses: Brie, Camembert, Gourmandaise, Crema Danica

    Semisoft cheeses: Bel Paese, Port Salut, Fontina, Muenster, Smoked Mozzarella

    Firm cheeses: Cheddar, Edam, Swiss or Gruyère, Gouda, Provolone

    "Moldy" cheeses: Roquefort, Blue (or Bleu), Gorgonzola

All cheeses should be served at room temperature, and you should be sure that the ripening cheeses like Brie and Camembert are fully mature and ready for serving when you buy them. (They will be a bit oozy when ripe.) To complete your buffet, serve interesting breads and crackers—dark pumpernickel, French or Italian bread, rye and wheat crackers, salty breadsticks. With these, you can fill out the table with fruit sections—apples, pears, grape clusters—and/or small bowls of black and green olives, cherry tomatoes, hot pickled Tuscan peppers. If you wish, you can also serve a variety of different sausages, sliced thin, to make an almost complete meal out of your cold buffet.

- No matter what you serve, try not to serve anything that has a critical timing that will have to be watched over after your guests arrive. There are so many variables that could throw off your schedule, and this is one headache that can be avoided.

- You should know in advance how many guests you can accommodate comfortably. (The number is sometimes dictated by a thing as mundane as the number of plates you have!) If necessary, most metropolitan areas have places that rent glasses and dinnerware at a modest fee. Strangely enough, some of them charge almost as much for delivery and pickup as they do for rental, so find out in advance what these charges are, and if you want to economize, go and get them yourself or delegate the responsibility to a friend or family member.

- The cardinal rule is: Have fun at your own party! If you are really enjoying yourself, your enthusiasm and hospitality will more than compensate for unmatched silverware or a lump or two in the gravy. Assuming that close friends will be there, take them up on their offers of assistance. It will leave you freer to deal with the inevitable minor crises that occur.

- Whenever possible, do everything you can the day before the party, or at least begin preparations which can be easily accomplished with no strain before guests arrive. Chances are, when you are running late, everyone will arrive right on the dot, so try to be ready for them.

3
A Kitchen on the Go

There are so many times when bringing food along on a trip can make a great difference. With the proliferation of fast-food chains across the country, those wonderful country restaurants, with their home-cooked meals, are becoming rarer and rarer. A trip along any of the toll roads and super highways can subject you to a culinary outrage that definitely does not make getting there part of the fun. Bringing your own food can also cut down time spent waiting for service, especially on summer weekends. If there are facilities along the way, plan to stop for lunch or supper at a roadside shelter, and barbecue steaks or hamburgers. It can be a real joy, and the economy of it makes good sense, too.

The tailgate picnic before sporting events is also rapidly becoming part of American culture, when crowds in restaurants make eating a struggle rather than a pleasure.

As more and more people take to the open road in trailers and campers, the frontier spirit that once marked America is returning. Your camper can also become the base of operations for a backpacking trip in the surrounding area, with each person bringing part of the meal to be made in the wild.

Boating has never been more popular, and there is nothing like a clear day and a fresh breeze blowing off the water to whet appetites. Galley cooking tests the ingenuity and organization of the chef, but a tranquil dinner aboard, with calm seas lapping against the hull and the setting sun as a backdrop, is a joy worth almost any effort.

A little preparation can add so much to your vacation enjoyment. You don't have to sacrifice your ordinary standards of living just because you are away from home. The added ingredient of fresh air can do more for a meal than a whole encyclopedia of sauces.

The Great Getaway

Happily, whether you go on a picnic or a fishing trip, camping in the mountains or for a weekend on a boat, most of the essential foods and cooking utensils you will need are the same. The first steps can be done at your leisure, before you plan to go away. Of course, the extent of your preparations will be determined by whether your trip will be a short or long one, an occasional one or a regular part of your lifestyle. If you camp regularly or own a boat, for example, it makes sense to have a permanent supply of utensils and food storage units that you can replenish as things are used or freshen up at the beginning of each season. Whatever your destination, you should try to conserve space and cut down on weight. (Naturally, these considerations will differ depending on where you are going and how you plan to get there.)

It is really remarkable to see how lightly people who travel as a way of life can pack, without any real sacrifice to comfort. The traveling kitchen is much like any other baggage a traveler brings—it is surprising how many things you really don't need. This is, of course, doubly true for the traveling larder. Keep it simple and you'll be a lot better off—especially if you will have to carry things for any distance. Many of those comforting jars and bottles back home on the kitchen shelf should stay there. Often, they are just a security blanket for nervous cooks. Don't bring them and you'll probably be a lot better off!

Try to plan your food needs as carefully as you plan your destination—they can be almost as important, and you will avoid the wasteful necessity of buying things you already have at home. Whenever practical, bring along as much as you can from home, picking up perishables near your destination. First of all, it makes good sense to shop in the neighborhood stores with which you are familiar. Then, when you get to your destination, you won't have to waste your leisure time ferreting out cooking needs. Another consideration is economy. If you are bound for a seasonal resort, chances are the stores will charge higher prices than you are used to paying at home.

If you are going to be out of doors, choose a traveling larder or food storage hamper that is light, capacious, and waterproof. if you care about appearances, the large wicker hampers are very attractive. To make them waterproof, line with a double layer of heavy-duty plastic garbage bags. If you have room in your car, station wagon, or camper, one of the best choices is an army footlocker, a camp trunk, or an old-fashioned steamer trunk, used on its side. They are meant for abuse and are almost indestructible. (I bought one in a pawnship once for a few dollars. It had ample room for all the supplies I needed, and fit perfectly into the trunk of my car.) If you plan regular trips, you can get a set of utensils and dinnerware that remain inside from trip to trip, making this part of going away that much easier.

Perishables can be dealt with just as easily. Inexpensive plastic foam coolers, in a variety of sizes, are available in supermarkets and discount stores. Use one for your fresh fruits and vegetables, soft drinks and beer. To avoid mildew, spray the inside with a disinfectant from time to time, and store the cooler uncovered when not in use. The most efficient way to pack a cooler is to use the frozen foods as refrigerants. Freeze orange juice in quart-size milk cartons, for example, and use them instead of ice cubes or commercial freezer packs, which will serve no other function. Use individually wrapped frozen steaks in the same way. Place the frozen foods around the edges. Then pack vegetables, butter, milk, and other perishables in the order of their use and fragility, putting the things you will use first on the top and in the center.

Obviously, if your trip is a short one and you don't want to spend the money, just pack your things in a clean, sturdy cardboard box (preferably from a liquor store). This may sound strange, but these boxes are often lined with a waterproof film to prevent spoilage of other bottles if one breaks in transit, and they are preferable to grocery boxes, which can sometimes have insects in them. To be safe, these may also be lined with plastic.

The next step is an essential but an easy one. Outfit your traveling larder with stackable plastic containers that can be nested when not in use. They are available virtually everywhere at low cost. (*They must have snug, snap-on lids* to avoid spillage and to keep the foods inside crisp and fresh.) I prefer square ones, which pack together snuggly, keeping things from jostling when in transit. They have the added advantage of being easy to store between trips. One of your purchases may be a large vegetable crisper, again with a tight snap-on lid. If it is large enough, it can also be packed with ice to hold the fish you catch until they are prepared.

Store your staples—flour, sugar, rice, pasta, coffee, crackers—in these tightly sealed containers. In humid areas, stacked cookies and crackers with inner wrappings have a better chance of staying crisp. Imported cookies, crackers, and biscuits packed in tins keep very well. They are more expensive, but generally are very good and the tins can be reused. Salt and pepper shakers should be tightly capped, although I think freshly ground pepper is so much better that it is worthwhile to bring along a small pepper mill.

Damp and humid air is the enemy of herbs, spices, and seasonings, so bring along only small quantities and you will have less to throw away at the end of your trip. Check the recipes you plan to make, and take only those seasonings you know you'll need. Keep them away from light in tightly closed bottles if possible, rather than cans or boxes, which absorb moisture more easily.

As you buy provisions, transfer only the amounts you will need for your trip to their appropriate plastic containers. Store the rest, and throw away any empty boxes at home. You can identify contents with a permanent marking pen or self-stick label. (Bringing just what you need lightens the load and conserves space; throwing away whatever refuse you can at home simplifies garbage disposal on your trip and helps to keep the campsite or recreation area unspoiled.)

Buy soft drinks and beer in cans instead of bottles. They weigh less and, of course, are unbreakable. It is also a good idea to buy a set of plastic bottles to store liquids and sauces. Be sure they have caps or screw-on tops that fit securely. Put these into an unused soda or beer six-pack carton and you will have a convenient traveling condiment shelf. The basic shopping list for food staples will vary with individual needs and preferences, but be sure to leave room for your personal follies—macadamia nuts, pickled pig's feet, whatever. (Often, when more than one person shops for a group, it turns into a major production without anyone getting what he or she wants, so make a shopping list beforehand and stick to it.) You should consider the following items for any kitchen on the go:

Bacon: In slab or canned form it keeps longer, and you also can use the rendered fat for braising meat, frying eggs.

Bisquick: In addition to or instead of flour. Use it for spoon bread, muffins, pancakes.

Bouillon cubes: Chicken and beef. Instant stock for cooking as well as for hot drinks and soup.

Dry soup: Get several varieties of the single-serving kind.

Bread: Rye and firm whole wheat hold up better than white.

Cheeses: Get the firmer ones—Cheddar, Swiss, Gouda—which keep better.

Eggs: The dry forms are kind of nasty, but they are better than nothing. Fresh eggs are best, but they take up space and are fragile; if you bring them, plunging them in their shells into boiling water for ten seconds will make them keep longer.

Margarine or butter: Margarine will keep better than butter; try for the soft margarine in plastic tubs.

Milk: If you are going for any length of time, get condensed or evaporated milk; if the weather is warm, you'll be better off with powdered.

Freeze-dried onions, garlic, shallots, mushrooms, bacon bits, chives: They lighten the load and are good for cooking.

Jams and jellies: If weight is a problem, buy single-serving packages.

Honey, corn, or maple syrup: Use instead of sugar on fruit, cereal, pancakes; sprinkle a little maple syrup on bacon a minute before it finishes cooking.

Lemon or lime juice: There is now frozen lemon juice available in a plastic bottle (Minute Maid brand). Otherwise, get reconstituted juice for salads, lemonade.

Tea, coffee, and cocoa: Take a survey of the preferences of your group—someone may need decaffeinated coffee, for example. Fresh ground coffee adds bulk, but if you are a coffee nut, you will want to bring it.

Peanut butter: Not only for the kids; a good source of protein.

Snack foods: Bring candy if you must, but nuts, raisins, dates, and other dried fruits are compact, delicious, and better for you. Get small individual packages if possible—they are easier to pack and keep fresher,

Sugar: A small box or individual packets.

Vegetables: Fresh vegetables are much tastier, but you can bring dehydrated or canned ones if necessary. Carrots, cabbage, cauliflower, broccoli, and celery keep well, and there is nothing like whole fresh potatoes, onions, corn, or yams baked in the coals of a campfire.

Naturally, you could go with a traveling version of a four-star restaurant, and if you have the room and the inclination, no one is going to stop you. If not, the list of basic kitchen appliances and utensils on pages 11–23 should carry you through with flying colors. You probably will not need everything. Consider it primarily as a checklist for what you have and what you will need.

Choose carefully, making as many things as possible serve two or more purposes. One common oversight is to forget to bring a really big pot with a snug-fitting cover. This should be a generous, 6- to 8-quart, lightweight, aluminum or stainless steel "spaghetti" pot. you'll end up using it to wash vegetables, mix salads, rinse dishes—as well as for its intended purpose of boiling corn on the cob, lobster, soup, and stew. To save space, it will hold a nest of graduated smaller pots inside. For the great outdoors, you should also consider the following items:

    Charcoal and starter
    Waterproof matches or lighter
    Barbecue grill or hibachi
    Tongs
    Skewers for kebobs
    Long-handled fork
    Heavy-duty aluminum foil
    Large heavy-duty plastic garbage bags
    Water purifier tablets
    Kerosene lantern or battery-operated light
    Basic tool set, including pliers, screwdriver, hammer, ax, shears
    Insect repellent
    First-aid kit
    A good fire extinguisher

At the risk of preaching, let me advise you to minimize the use of paper plates and other disposables unless you know you will have an easy way to dispose of them. We have all been in places of great natural beauty that have been spoiled by the discarded debris of careless people who have preceded us. Be a sport and help preserve the ecology of the places you visit. (And you can also save money, since paper and plastic throwaways are expensive when their brief life span is considered.)

Attractive sets of unbreakable dishes, glasses, and flatware, in handsome, specially fitted hampers, are available at fancy department and specialty stores. Much less expensive but perfectly serviceable versions can be purchased at most sporting goods and department stores, as well as from camping outfitters. You can also assemble your own quite simply at a local houseware store. Buy unbreakable tumblers and hot-drink mugs that nest one into another for compact storage. Any large household goods store will have a handsome array of inexpensive high-impact plastic or other unbreakable dinnerware that will do nicely. When choosing flatware, try to get a set with knives that have serrated blades. They can serve as table, steak, and utility knives, saving unnecessary duplication.

Campsite Cooking

Whether we go off in a fully equipped camper or throw some things in the back of the car and take off for parts known or unknown, Americans are on the move. Perhaps it is a resurgence of our frontier spirit—getting back out into the wilderness. Whatever the reason, more and more of us are getting away—renewing our contact with the world around us, sleeping under the stars, and recharging our spiritual batteries.

Since there are many excellent guides to the various facets of outdoor living and cooking, I will simply offer a few common-sense suggestions on how to make life under the open sky a bit more civilized.

Two basic rules remain constant for all outdoor situations. The first and most important is: Plan ahead! There is nothing more disconcerting than getting out into the wilderness the discovering that something essential has been forgotten—like fuel for the camp stove, or aluminum foil (which is the campfire cook's best friend). The second basic rule is that utensils and foodstuffs must be compact and portable. Everything should serve at least two purposes—the little amenities of life become secondary when they have to be carried, unpacked and repacked time after time.

A backpacking trip in the mountains, however, requires a different set of game plans than a family camping trip to a state or national park, where facilities are available for more or less conventional living, just roughing it a bit.

When traveling long distances on foot, every ounce of extra weight will feel like a pound in no time. If you are backpacking, provisions and utensils must be considerably curtailed. The best approach is to get to the nearest camping outfitter that caters to climbers and backpackers and buy one of the mess kits available for just this purpose. Bring along as many dehydrated foods as possible. Many camping outfitters also carry—or will be able to tell you where to get—special meals that are completely prepared and ready to add water, heat and eat. The advent of freeze-dried foods is a boon to the camper, especially the backpacker. Today, dozens of dried and freeze-dried foods are available. They vary in quality—some things are remarkably close to their natural equivalents, others are a dismal failure. Everyone is familiar with powdered and freeze-dried instant coffee; I think the freeze-dried kind is better, but choose what suits your own taste.

Another primary consideration in backpacking is water. If you are going to an unfamiliar area or one where there may be a shortage of safe water, bring along a supply of pills such as Bursoline and Halazone that can make water drinkable. You should, of course, carry a canteen (as large as possible) and fill it whenever possible.

Family camping isn't all that different from picnicking these days, except it's usually longer (and you can't take the dishes home to wash). Campsite cooking, naturally, can be much more substantial than preparing food when on a backpacking trip. Part of your preparedness should be to try at least a few of the major recipes you plan to use at home before setting out. (This is not to demean your abilities, but if something is going to be a disaster, it is better to have it happen at home when there are stores nearby.) When possible, make dishes that are more complicated or take a long time at home and freeze them, or plan to use them on your first dinner away from home.

If you are really roughing it and don't want to bother with much cooking on the first night, bring a few canned foods and

A KITCHEN ON THE GO 37

heat them in their cans. (This works best with uncondensed soups, stews, chili, and water-packed vegetables.) Be sure to take the label off and open the can before heating. If you will be traveling in a camper or station wagon, investigate the possibilities of a covered cast iron kettle on three legs. Set it in the coals of a campfire (and place a few coals on the lid), and it will serve as a baking oven for making casseroles, stews, roasting chickens, and meats. If you have the room, a percolator will come handy. Use it not only for coffee, but to boil water for tea, instant soup and hard-cooked eggs.

Be sure to bring a large roll of heavy-weight aluminum foil. Use it to line a frying pan and you will have one less pan to wash. Wrap foil around scrubbed potatoes, onions in their skins, cored apples, and husked corn to be roasted in the embers of a charcoal fire. (You can also roast corn in its husk in the embers—first removing the silk and reclosing the husks.) Package eviscerated fish, along with butter, margarine, or oil and herbs, in foil for roasting in the coals; use the foil as a reflector cover for pan biscuits. To reflect the heat upward and make a hotter fire, put foil under the coals in a makeshift charcoal pit. Frozen meats wrapped in aluminum foil keep cold much longer.

You can also make use of the compartmented aluminum pans available in supermarkets to heat several things at the same time. Crimp an aluminum foil cover around the top to keep the food from drying out while it is heating on the grill or fire. An aluminum or stainless steel skewer inserted into a baking potato or a roast will make it cook faster.

Try a few tricks with coffee. Instant coffee adds a piquant flavor when sprinkled on broiling meat and, believe it or not, a teaspoon of instant coffee added to the water when boiling rice gives it a distinctive, nutty taste. Try making hobo coffee: Put a heaping tablespoon of ground coffee for each cup of cold water in a sauce pan—a pinch of salt helps, but only one pinch for the whole potful. Boil for three to five minutes and strain through a clean cloth (a clean white sock, if you have nothing else).

When camping beside a stream, put perishables, in tightly

closed plastic bags, inside a nylon mesh bag and keep them submerged, with a stone inside the bag for weight. If you have the energy and plan to stay in one place for a while, old trail-blazers say that a three-foot-deep pit will keep food cool when covered by earth. Store the food in a tin or plastic bag and cover with a canvas or plastic sheet before replacing the dirt.

As you walk through woods and fields, you will find an entire salad garden underfoot if you look for it. You can eat tender young dandelion leaves, sorrel, ferns, violet leaves and blossoms (an exotic and lovely topping for the dark greens), clover leaves and blossoms, and wild onions. In the late spring, wild watercress—a delicious green with a slightly peppery taste—can sometimes be found in the neighborhood of overflowing streams. Use these alone or combine them with the more usual salad ingredients, with a simple classic French vinaigrette dressing (page 76) or oil and vinegar to complement the delicate flavors. Look for wild berries as well—blueberries, strawberries, blackberries, elderberries, raspberries—and perhaps you can get to them before the birds do.

If you want to try your hand at foraging for food in the wild, there are many interesting books available to help you identify edible greens and berries. Bring one of them along with you and *never* eat anything unless you are absolutely sure of what it is. Unless you really are an expert, stay away from *all* mushrooms, no matter how well they seem to match the illustrations in books.

Splendor in the Grass: Picnics and Movable Feasts

The weather is fine and there's a big yellow sun in the sky; what better reason for a picnic at the beach, off the tailgate of the station wagon, or in your own backyard. With fresh air as the mysterious secret ingredient, everything always tastes so much better.

This can be the most satisfying kind of cooking without a kitchen. It gives the chef a respite—eating out-of-doors with family or friends willing to pitch in, when ordinarily they wouldn't budge! Even if a little prodding is required, make it a group effort: no work, no food.

Plan your meal so that at least some of the work can be done at home ahead of time. I have included many recipes that can be made in advance and are well suited to outdoor eating. Make a hearty entrée like chili—with a corn bread topping (page 141); baked in a heavy casserole and wrapped in aluminum foil, it will hold its heat for several hours until you are ready to eat. Or try a savory beef stew or lasagna. Just make a salad and a simple dessert like brownies or fresh fruit, with cold beer or jug wine to drink, and you'll have a complete and satisfying meal.

Even if you want to barbecue your food on the spot (pages 129–131) try to do as much as you can beforehand. Wash and shake salad greens dry, wrap in paper towels to catch the extra moisture, and put them in a plastic bag to keep crisp. If hamburgers (page 130) are your choice, make the patties beforehand and pack them in aluminum foil, ready for grilling. Kebobs (page 129) that are cooked over a charcoal fire are perfect for a picnic, and the preparations can be done at home. Plan to make use of the coals for more than just grilling the meat. Vegetables can be wrapped in aluminum foil and cooked in the coals along with the rest of the meal. Coffee can be made on top.

For a more elaborate picnic, bring along a selection of appetizers (pages 88–98). Try to make your choice from the sturdy finger foods that can be made ahead of time. Asparagus, steamed beforehand and wrapped with thinly sliced boiled ham, makes a delicious picnic dish. Bring along a Classic French Vinaigrette dressing (page 76) and add it when you serve with some interesting rolls or French bread.

If you are feeling lazy, you can put together a more than credible picnic with provisions from the supermarket or delicatessen and a little imagination. Many markets have barbecued chickens and spareribs ready for eating, as well as a wide selection of salads already made and sauced. (In summer, do not get foods made with mayonnaise unless you can keep them cold until you are ready to eat—they spoil readily and can make you deathly ill.)

Depending on where you can shop, your meal could run the gamut from Italian hero or submarine sandwiches to a *fête champêtre* with champagne, smoked salmon, rare roast beef, French Brie cheese and fruit for dessert.

If you want sandwiches on your menu, they won't be limp and soggy if you bring the fixings and make the sandwiches when you are ready to eat.

The Chef at Sea

Cooking aboard a boat is governed by rules and limitations that do not apply to other kitchens on the go. Planning and organization are the heart and soul of the galley cook's success. Decide in advance how much cooking you will need to do on board, and plan your menus with the meticulousness of a general about to make an important battle decision. Make a list of all provisions and supplies you are likely to need and try to buy and stow them aboard in advance—you probably won't want the bother of stopping to pick up provisions once you get under way.

Anticipate any variables—unexpected hungry guests or an extra day of sailing—by setting aside a few emergency rations. Canned tuna, sardines, or a small ham, dates and raisins, canned fruit drinks (or the powdered concentrates) and soft drinks can be stowed away for this eventuality. A supply of snack foods is always handy. Tinned nuts, hard cheese (Cheddar and Swiss), fruits and carrots, will keep hungry sailors quiet until mealtime. The general advice for all outdoor cooking given earlier—about storing everything in tightly sealed plastic containers or tins—applies doubly to the humid conditions on the water.

The basic principle of effective cooking on board is to spend as little time in the galley as possible. Your stove may be mounted on gimbals, pivoted supports that keep the stove level when the boat is rolling, preventing (theoretically) everything from sliding off. Even so, you probably will want to keep an eye on the pots while they're cooking—an ounce of prevention is worth a meal on the floor or a fire in the cabin. This means your galley *must* be equipped with a good marine fire extinguisher (the foam and carbon dioxide types are most effective). Keep curtains, towels, and any other flammable items well away from your stove; and you must keep everything spotless. Cleanliness on a boat is not merely a virtue, it is an absolute necessity. Spilled grease or fuel, messy in any circumstances, can be deadly on board.

It also means you must choose your foods carefully. Naturally, because of the danger of fire, you should not deep-fry foods aboard. And if you make slow, long-cooking dishes, you will be cooped up in the galley, making meal preparation tedious—the last thing you want on a pleasure trip. Anything complicated should be made beforehand. No one need be aware that there is any difference between your complete kitchen at home and your little on-board galley—and you'll be able to spend more time on deck in the sun. For hungry salts, you could serve flavorful, filling casseroles, pasta and rice dishes, or a whole variety of stews made ahead of time at home from the recipes that follow (even frozen, if you like) for quick reheating on board.

Because of space limitations, keep salads to the more compact variety—tomatoes and cucumbers, fruit salads, raw chewy vegetables like celery and carrots (which are not fragile and can be served and stored with ease). Use canned condensed milk instead of fresh for coffee and tea. Omelets and other egg dishes are ideal luncheon suggestions because they are so quick and easy to prepare. If anyone has caught fish that day, you have the perfect seashore dinner.

One seasoned sailing couple I know suggest using a pressure cooker for reheating frozen or precooked foods on board, with the cover fastened securely, but the pressure control off. Add twice the liquid required—steam will vent and you can cook in a conventional manner; and if the boat pitches suddenly, nothing will spill.

If you have a refrigerator on board, so much the better. If not, use a plastic foam cooler for perishables, organizing the packing for maximum efficiency as described in the general discussion earlier.

Try to use multipurpose utensils and cookware, such as casseroles that can go from the refrigerator or freezer to the oven and then to the table. Paper plates and disposable tableware can be used for a short weekend trip if you hate washing dishes or have no facilities on board. If boating is more than an occasional pastime, you need a set of unbreakable dishes. Make sure to get plates, tumblers, and heavy mugs that are sturdy enough to withstand the rough use they will encounter on board. To conserve drinking water, you can wash dishes in clean water (salt or fresh) brought up in a bucket from over the side.

Here is a typical menu to show you how to organize a weekend on board with a minimum of trouble. The more substantial dishes can be cooked on shore and reheated on board or at a marina.

Friday Dinner
Breast of Chicken Orientale
   (pages 167–168)
Rice
Fruit salad with rum or kirsch
Tea or beer

Saturday Breakfast
Bacon Omelet (page 123)
Orange juice
English muffins
Coffee, tea, or milk

Saturday Lunch
Gazpacho (pages 101–102)
Asparagus and Ham
   Vinaigrette (page 172)
White wine
Fresh fruit and cheese

Saturday Dinner

Chili Casserole with Corn Bread Topping (pages 139–141)
Sliced tomatoes with Classic French Vinaigrette Dressing (page 76)
Cold beer
Brownies or cookies

Sunday Brunch

Cantaloupe
Curried Tuna Salad (page 116)
Cucumbers with Dill Dressing (page 77)
Coffee, tea, or milk

4
Getting It Together

The Basics

Think of the best cook you know. Chances are, there are two or three specialties that you really hope will be served on your next visit. Doing anything well is a matter of developing skills, of practice combined with flair, and food is no exception. If you learn a few basic techniques and approach cooking with confidence and imagination, you are certain to become known for your own specialties.

One of the essentials of good food is the personality and preferences of the chef. This is the reason why certain restaurants are so-so while others become world famous, although they might be serving almost identical menus.

When you try a new recipe, you should begin by doing it "by the book." Then, as you become familiar with the recipe and more confident repeating it, you may want to add your own personal touches—a bit more butter, a dash of red pepper, a splash of sherry at the last moment. That, I admit, is how I learned to cook: I followed the recipes with scientific accuracy until I learned them down to the tips of my fingers. Then, as they became more natural, I was able to create short cuts and subtle variations that made them my own.

You may not feel comfortable enough in the kitchen to start improvising for a while—perhaps never. But you should try to develop the self-assurance to make a dish your very own, just as the great chefs of the world have made their own variations the accepted rule. I think you'll find cooking much more fun that way.

Even if the closest contact you've had with foreign food is the dinner scene in the movie *Tom Jones,* don't be put off by dishes with exotic-sounding names. After all, practically everything in American cooking started as a foreign food—from spaghetti and pizza to frankfurters and omelets. Actually, these glamorous foreign names often describe dishes that are very familiar and easy to prepare. Stews, for example, are part of practically every cuisine in the world, and nothing could be simpler to make. Basically, just meat or fish simmered slowly with vegetables. Every cuisine has its own particular combinations of ingredients and little variations—and, of course, its own particular names—but it's all stew. So you'll feel a little less intimidated, here's a brief list of stews by their foreign names, with the special ingredients that make each one unique.

BEEF STEWS
Boeuf Bourguignon (French, with red wine, vegetables and herbs)
Beef Stroganoff (Russian, with sour cream)
Carbonnades à la Flamande (Flemish, with beer)
Cholent (Jewish, with onions and dried beans)
Vindaloo (Indian, with vinegar and hot spices)
Goulash (Hungarian, with paprika, potatoes, carrots, tomato paste)

CHICKEN STEWS
Poulet au pot (French, steamed with vegetables in broth)
Jewish chicken soup (really a watery stew with onions, carrots)
Pollo alla cacciatore (Italian, with tomatoes, wine, mushrooms)
Chicken fricassee (American, stewed with vegetables in a creamy sauce)
Pollo mole de Guajolote (Mexican, with chili pepper and chocolate!)
Arroz con pollo (Spanish, baked with saffron rice, tomatoes, and pimientoes)

FISH STEWS

Bouillabaisse (French, with mixed saltwater fish and shellfish)
Peixe a moda de Alentejo (Portuguese, with potatoes)
Cacciucco (Italian, mixed fish and shellfish with a peppery garlic sauce)
Creole gumbo (New Orleans style, with shellfish and okra)

So you see, it is all relative. One man's fish, (if you'll pardon the pun) is a Frenchman's *poisson*. Once you become familiar with the elementary skills of preparation and cooking, you can serve the most exotic-sounding foods with ease, and with a real feeling of accomplishment. See Chapter 20, "The Language of Cooking."

The world's cuisines evolved from foodstuffs that were native to each particular area. There is a great deal of overlapping, of course, because natural environments influence cooking more strongly than national boundaries. Thus, northern Italian cooking resembles French cuisine more than it does Neapolitan; the cooking of Mediterranean Marseilles has more affinity with the pungent foods of Spain than with the refined haute cuisine of Paris. The English and Dutch recipes that the Pilgrims brought from Europe were altered by the native foods of the New World. Corn, wild turkey, sweet potatoes, and tomatoes all came from the Americas and were incorporated into the cuisines of the mother countries. Colonization and exploration, trade and travel all over the world, from the first Phoenicians to soldiers returning from Vietnam, has brought about a cross-pollination of cuisines that is truly remarkable.

The food of America is a particularly happy mélange of tastes and flavors, with the whole world contributing to its culinary vocabulary. Such an embarrassment of riches often makes it difficult to decide exactly what to cook and how to prepare it. From my own experience, I offer the following advice: When in doubt, make it fresh and keep it simple.

When making your cooking plans, freshness should always determine what you will serve. Do this, and you cannot go wrong.

Consider what seasonal foods, and particularly what locally grown produce and fruits, may be available. Take advantage of them while they are around. You can eat the canned, frozen, or the hothouse-grown foods any time, but in most parts of the country snappy fresh green beans and cucumbers, sun-ripened tomatoes, newly picked sweet young corn and soft-shelled crabs (to give only a few examples) are around for only a short time each year. Buy fresh herbs when you see them; they're so much nicer than the dried ones. (If you have a green thumb and a sunny window, you may consider growing your own herbs.) Keep a mental calendar of when locally grown strawberries and blueberries, peaches and plums, make their appearances so you'll remember to watch out for them. Watch out, too, for some of the meats and fish that are seasonal (like spring lamb and oysters) or simply not always available (like fresh fish of many kinds).

The great chef Escoffier once remarked, "Food must taste of itself." This is another basic rule of good cooking: Great food requires great simplicity. If this sounds obvious, just stop for a minute and think of all the times you have eaten a bad meal that started out with perfectly good ingredients. It is a mistake (and unfortunately a common one) to confuse complicated food with expertise. The difference between ordinary cooking and fine cuisine is not necessarily a matter of progressing from simple dishes to elaborately prepared ones. One of the grandest houses of the nineteenth century used to hire chefs on the strength of how they prepared a simple leg of lamb. Anyone with interest and time can learn how to make a sauce, but it takes an artist to know when to leave well enough alone.

When planning a meal, make sure that the various dishes and courses do not conflict with one another. Serving a creamy soup, rich or spicy entrée, heavy salad dressing, and rich dessert will not only bore the palate, it will put your guests to sleep. Besides, trying to put together such a series of dishes all at the same time, in a small kitchen—or none at all—can cause a nervous breakdown! If you want to serve a very complex or highly seasoned dish, do yourself and your guests a favor: make it the star of the dinner and let the rest of the meal act as the supporting players in the drama. An involved main dish, for instance, asks for a crunchy green salad, perhaps some homemade or brown-and-serve bread, and a simple dessert. Fruit and cheese are the perfect conclusion to a fine meal, and nothing could be easier. All you have to do is arrange the fruit in a bowl and remember to take the cheese out of the refrigerator well before you serve so it will be at room temperature when you're ready for dessert.

If you learn the discipline of planning ahead, you will have mastered one of the most fundamental of all rules of good cooking. For anyone who has to work in a small or makeshift kitchen, careful planning is not only important, it is the first rule of survival. Especially when entertaining, try to organize a menu that leaves you free to spend time with your family or friends before serving—one that won't keep you cooking while everyone else is eating. This isn't as hard as you may think.

Plan the dishes and courses of your meal according to their complexity and the time required for preparation. Do your shopping earlier if you can. Check recipe instructions not only for length of cooking time, but to see what can be done in advance. Don't have a meal that requires too many things that have to be done at the last minute. Many dishes require no cooking at all, and some can be partially or completely cooked well ahead of time and reheated for a few minutes just before you're ready to bring them to the table. Many entrées even improve with reheating. Consider dishes that can be left to cook untended—thick peasant soups and roasts, for example—allowing you to concentrate on preparing something else or to enjoy a cocktail with your guests. Salad ingredients can be rinsed and dried on paper towels in advance and stored in a plastic bag in the refrigerator. My "house" dressing is a classic French vinaigrette (page 76). It's simple to put together, and I like to mix it in the bottom of the salad bowl directly before serving. The salad is easier to toss this way, and there is one less dish to wash.

When you are cooking without a kitchen, you must have the logistical abilities of a scientist. The number of dishes you will have to wash may not be the primary consideration in planning a menu, but it is one of them. Do check to be sure you won't need to use your one large pot for two different things at the same time. The same advice applies to your oven, your electric frying pan, the burners of your stove (or hot plate), in fact, to any appliance you may be using. Also, if possible, table settings, silverware, and serving dishes and pieces should be organized well in advance.

Another aspect of good planning is to assemble all your ingredients before you begin to prepare a recipe. Don't laugh. Many an experienced cook, myself included, has made something they know by heart, only to remember when it is too late that some essential ingredient is missing. Especially if your work space is small, clear away anything unnecessary before you start to cook, and try to wash your utensils as you go along, getting them out of the way as you proceed. In tight quarters, clutter can spell ruin. You'll probably have to use some of your utensils for more than one purpose anyway (the colander for washing salad greens can become the steamer for your vegetables). You'll feel much less harried if your tools are ready when you need them.

A proper chopping block is also a great help. If space is a problem, you can buy or make a hardwood cutting board that will fit over your sink, with a hole sawed out at one end through which to push discarded vegetable parings, trimmed fat, and bones. When cutting foods for cooking, remember that cooking time is determined by the density of foods and the penetration of heat. The thinner or smaller the pieces, the faster the meal is made. This is the secret of the delicious stir-fried foods of the Orient.

Always preheat your oven to the full temperature called for in your recipe. This usually takes ten to fifteen minutes. It is important to keep the level of heat constant, so open the oven as little as possible. When basting or testing for doneness, do it quickly and be sure to close (or cover) your oven door completely. This is especially crucial when baking cakes, breads, and soufflés.

Some things should be cooked from a cold start. Place eggs to be boiled in cold salted water before turning on the heat. Start bacon in a cold frying pan and cook slowly to prevent sticking and to minimize shrinkage. When you want to boil water, cover the pot and it will come to a boil more quickly (and save fuel or electricity). Adding salt to water raises the boiling point of the water, allowing foods to cook more rapidly.

Do try to use ingredients at the proper temperature. For cooking (and especially baking), most ingredients should be at room temperature for best results. It is a hell of a lot harder to cream together butter and sugar if the butter is straight from the refrigerator and hard as a rock. Recipes will usually indicate any unusual temperature requirements. If you are going to make a frozen fowl, read the wrapper, which will tell you how long the bird will take to thaw. (Some of the larger turkeys seem to be left over from the last Ice Age and take forever to thaw, so be sure to check in advance.)

Frozen fruits often come in "quick-thaw" plastic envelopes. If you leave the fruit at room temperature after shopping, it should be ready by dessert time. Personally, I like some fruit slightly frozen—see Minty Pineapple Slush (page 205).

One rule about wine is that there is no rule about wine. A wine connoisseur once corrected my observation that room temperature was the proper way to serve red wines. He felt they should be served at "cellar" temperature (56 to 58 degrees), or at the particular preference of the host or guests. In other words, do as you please. Chances are, like most people, you'll want to serve a red wine with beef, white wine to complement the more delicate flavor of chicken and fish. I prefer beer with highly seasoned chili or Indian curries, but wine is just as good. There are so many "experts" on the subject, however, that one can easily go through life following set after set of iron-clad rules and recommendations and never repeat the same vintage. Therefore, if you like it, drink it!

Tricks of the Trade

Sometimes it does pay to throw the rule books away. In food as in life, the unexpected, the element of surprise, can delight the senses and the palate. The easiest things can be elevated to the level of haute cuisine simply by varying the proportions, or by clever combinations. The first person who thought of making gazpacho, the delicious salad-soup of Spain, merely added raw chopped tomatoes and other vegetables to a cold soup stock, a simple enough combination. Yet that unknown cook created something totally unusual, because the large proportion of vegetables to stock, the texture of raw rather than cooked vegetables, and the cold instead of hot temperature are unexpected.

I was once served an exquisite aspic with hard-cooked eggs inside. (Curiously, though gelatin desserts are standard fare everywhere, most Americans do not serve aspics.) Not until I actually cut into the eggs did I realize that they were not plain hard-cooked eggs at all, but deviled, held together with toothpicks. It is time consuming to prepare (pages 118–119), but it does have the quality of surprise that makes a memorable meal.

The interplay of hot and cold, sweet and sour, is better understood outside the United States than here at home. Hot Madras curries (pages 165 and 185) are accompanied by an array of side dishes—from fiery-hot peppers to cooling yogurt—that provide the most dazzling changes of taste and texture, all with the purpose of keeping the palate awake and interested. The Hungarians have a cold cherry soup (pages 107–108), a sweet beginning to a memorable meal. The cream stock is filled with tart pitted fruit, and the unexpected taste can set the tone of what is to follow.

Delightful dishes such as these may have been created on purpose, but just as often they are the happy results of accidents. Necessity, after all, is the true mother of invention. Remember that adage when you think you've made a disastrous mistake and are ready to toss it out and go to the local pizzeria. Before the "failure" goes into the garbage, make sure there is no way to rescue it. Even if the dish may come out differently than you originally intended, if it tastes all right serve it. Toast that you have burned and scraped is not dried up and overdone, it is Melba toast. So, if havoc strikes, take a deep breath and see if you can brazen it through. Who knows—they might love it!

If you really do ruin something and are stuck for a first course at the last minute, whip up a fast but authentic-tasting Chinese Egg Drop Soup. Just mix ½ a teaspoon of cornstarch with each cup cool water, combined with instant chicken broth or bouillon, bring it to a boil, and add a beaten egg as it boils rapidly. The cornstarch will thicken the broth and the shreds of egg will cook in the hot broth. Serve it with chopped chives or scallions. Voilà, another triumph!

Overcooked vegetables can be mashed or puréed in a food mill or blender (or even pushed through an ordinary sieve) and served as an elegant side dish. Whenever confronted, claim you did it on purpose!

Of course, you don't have to wait for accidents to happen to add extra-special touches to your cooking.

An easy trick for buttered spinach is to grate some fresh nutmeg on the top just before serving, tossing lightly with a fork to distribute the fragrant spice. You can also use finely grated hard-cooked egg—what the French call mimosa—as a garnish for the spinach. A little wire-handled grater, about the size of a playing card, is perfect for grating eggs or spices, as well as lemon peel and cheese. (They are available almost everywhere but, if you are keeping your utensils to a bare minimum, an old-fashioned four-sided "knuckle scraper" can do just about the same job.)

Another utensil that can help you achieve an extra dimension in food preparation is the simple potato peeler. Cucumbers shaved paper-thin in rounds with a potato peeler, instead of sliced in the usual manner, take on an extra delicacy—as do carrots, and other raw and cooked vegetables. The French prefer to remove the seeds of the cucumber, using only the outer flesh, but this is strictly a matter of personal preference. If you like eating the peel and are using cucumbers that have been coated with a wax, wash this off with soap before using. Cucumbers, yogurt, and mint leaves are combined in an especially interesting Middle Eastern salad (page 115)—again, a surprising and exotic taste.

Garlic provides a veritable grab bag of tricks of the trade—and here a sense of proportion truly is everything. An enthusiastic beginner will sometimes overdo the garlic and overpower an entire dish with it. The whole *bulb* of garlic, by the way, is segmented into *cloves*. This may be common knowledge, but it's worth repeating. I once gave a recipe for a French stew to a sweet young thing. It called for three cloves of garlic, but the instant she opened the door as I came to dinner I knew something was very wrong. She had used three *bulbs,* not three cloves, of garlic, and it was months before the smell left her apartment! When used with discretion (not to say diplomacy), however, garlic can be another of the cook's best friends. An ancient element in the cuisine of virtually every culture, it has been ascribed with marvelous powers—everything from curing colds and colic to keeping away vampires. Fresh garlic should be used whenever possible, either finely minced or put through a garlic press. You can also tie crushed garlic cloves in a piece of cheesecloth, to be removed from a soup or sauce after cooking. Slivers of garlic inserted, into a leg of lamb with rosemary is a classic seasoning for a classic dish, and the discreet inclusion of garlic in almost any Mediterranean dish is required by custom. Try rubbing a bruised clove of garlic around the inside of your wooden salad bowl before adding the dressing. The faint flavor adds zest to whatever greens you use. (Remember to discard the bruised garlic clove before tossing the salad.)

Try coarse kosher salt for cooking; for some mysterious reason it does a better job. Use it to salt meat and poultry—it is flaky and sticks well. It is also good as a pan-broiling agent: Pour a layer of kosher salt in the bottom of a frying pan, turn the heat on high, and when the pan is hot put steak or hamburgers on to cook. The salt seals in the juices, searing the meat to a crispy brown without making it overly salty.

If you *do* oversalt something cooking in liquid, add a cut-up raw potato and let it cook for 15 minutes. Then fish it out and some saltiness is reduced.

Progress marches on, and we are the beneficiaries, as well as the victims, of change. Today, strawberries are available all year long, as are many other fruits and vegetables. But the price we pay (and I don't mean only money) is dear. Tomatoes picked green for shipping over long distances taste wooden and pulpy; and many attractive and well-shaped fruits seem to have lost their fragrance and freshness in the process. Mealy fruit can sometimes be perked up with a few drops of lemon juice. Tossing strawberries and other berries with a little sugar before serving will coax out the flavorful juices and add to their taste. Or, if you have some tired fruit that does not pass muster for serving fresh, add a sliced orange or lemon (or both) to enhance the flavor and cook it with some raisins and sugar for a tasty fruit compote.

Lemons are the great secret weapon against all sorts of kitchen disasters. I put a squeeze or two of lemon juice on cut fresh fruit or fruit salad to keep it from turning brown. The peel of a lemon is a great sparkler for drinks of all kinds. An easy way to remove the peel without the flesh is to use a potato peeler. A drop or two of lemon juice (in the secrecy of your cooking area) added to cheap jug wine can sometimes tone down the cloying edge. (Naturally, lemon juice is not a panacea for everything—one can only do so much—but think of how great sangria tastes on a hot summer day.)

There is a common misconception that rice is hard to make. In fact, all you need is a pot with a good tight lid and a heat source low enough for simmering. (The lower the heat during cooking, the better your rice will be.) The rule of thumb is one part rice to two parts water. Salt the water and add a little butter or cooking oil to keep the grains separate. Or add flavor by substituting bouillon for all or part of the water. Use chicken stock with chicken dishes, beef broth with beef, or vegetable with other dishes.

Bouillon is the chef's "stock in trade." Also called stock, broth, and consommé, the subtle differences need not be elaborated, since the terms are usually used interchangeably (as they are here). The uses for stock are practically endless: Part of most soups and stews, it also adds a nice flavor to vegetables (use stock instead of water). You can make your own chicken or beef stock very easily (page 100) or use the commercial canned bouillon cube or powdered versions. If a recipe calls for fish stock, use the liquid in which you have poached fish (court bouillon, page 179) or substitute bottled clam juice.

When preparing a stock, one good way to be ahead of the game is to use the water from boiled or steamed vegetables to enrich the broth. Full of vitamins and flavor, you can dissolve bouillon cubes in it or add it to your stockpot. If you have room, a convenient way to store stock is to freeze it in an ordinary ice cube tray, then transfer the cubes to a plastic bag for storage in the freezer until needed. Generally, you won't even have to thaw them before using in cooking, and they are delicious used in Bloody Marys instead of regular ice!

Another trick of the trade involves soups as well. There are so many occasions when you are left with an awkward amount of meat or stew after dinner—too much to throw away and not really enough to save. With the ever-increasing price of food, one way to use these leftovers is in an old-fashioned homemade soup. There are several brands of dry soups that require long cooking (generally an hour and a half to two hours). Goodman's and Manischewitz are available in large chain markets. Since these are basically only combinations of ingredients with full cooking to be done, they seem to taste more homemade than many condensed soups. Varieties include Lima bean and barley, split pea and minestrone—all are tasty and all are very inexpensive. Simply make the soup according to directions and add your leftovers cut into small pieces (hopefully with some gravy) to the cooking pot a half hour before it is done. Served with crusty French or Italian bread and salad, it makes a fine meal for a cold blustery day.

Vinegar is one of the oldest food substances found on the kitchen shelf. Known for centuries as a universal preservative, there is a story (probably apocryphal) that Cleopatra once dissolved a huge pearl in vinegar in order to win a bet with Marc Antony over who could spend more on a dinner! Unlike Cleopatra, many people generally take vinegar for granted, using only one kind. There are several interesting varieties, and you might like to experiment with some of them. My own preference is for wine vinegar, which I use for most salad dressings. For pickling, try white vinegar. Cider vinegar is good if you want a tart, tangy taste. Tarragon-flavored vinegar is good in a salad, and garlic vinegar can be used in anything that calls for vinegar; or try one that is flavored with shallots or chives. These flavored vinegars are now available in many stores, but you can make them very easily and far more cheaply than you can buy them. Recipes are given on pages 75–76.

One little economy you might want to observe is to pour those few last drops of red wine left after dinner into your red wine vinegar bottle. It fortifies the taste and makes it more tangy.

One of my most favorite tricks of the trade is to use vodka as a base for special drinks and homemade liqueurs. For a summer drink, I like to take the peel of a whole juice orange or lemon (removing it in a single thin spiral with a potato peeler) and thread it through the neck of a bottle of vodka. Keep it in the freezer, and after a few days the vodka will be deliciously flavored and colored by the peel. It pours like maple syrup, and served neat, it can knock your socks off! But it is also fine in other mixed drinks. The Russians and Scandinavians serve shots of icy straight vodka with a flavorful appetizer like smoked salmon, pâté, or herring—anything with a distinctive flavor that could go with a strong drink.

Frozen cranberry or apple juice concentrate—thawed but not diluted—added to vodka makes a wonderful after-dinner drink at a fraction of the cost of a liqueur. Raspberry, strawberry, and other fruit syrups are also good. The proportions are up to you. Try experimenting and see what you like best.

Instead of the traditional martini, try pouring vodka on the rocks and adding a few *drops* of Pernod, Ricard, or other anise-based liqueurs, with a twist of lemon or orange peel. If you like a licorice-flavored drink, this one is very interesting and unusual.

The Russians have a whole range of flavored vodka and vodka-based drinks (Zubrovka is flavored with buffalo grass). They also like to sprinkle red or black pepper in their vodka—try that some time and see how you like it.

The Triumph of the Senses

All over the world, the taking of food together has implications that go far beyond maintaining life. "Breaking bread together," "The salt of the earth," "He takes the cake." Our speech is filled with references to food. In our customs, food is commonly used as a token of friendship and goodwill. Tribal societies are especially rich in such customs—if he takes food with them, even an enemy must be shown the same hospitality accorded an honored guest. Food plays a role in the rites and observances of every religion. Jews commemorate the Passover holiday with a ritual feast in which unleavened bread, bitter herbs, and wine have deep symbolic meaning. Muslims observe Ramadan with day-long fasts, followed by feasts in which special foods are served. And every Christian culture has its own Christmas and Easter foods, all serving as basic expressions of love and hospitality to family, friends, and neighbors.

At the other end of the scale is the harried mother who has too much to do and not enough time or help to do it, trying to plan and cook inventive and different family meals. My own feeling is that cooking should be thought of as an extension of what we believe and hope to accomplish in other areas. (Think of all those starving artists who ended up eating the still lifes that they have painted!)

Cooking and cuisine can be an art, a craft, or a disaster. It all depends on how you approach it and how much of yourself you put into it.

The making of food can be transformed from a drudgery into a kind of creative expression, if it is regarded as a sensual experience, one that involves color, smell, taste, texture, and sound—listening to sizzling steaks or popping corn makes one hungry. Once you take these different senses into account as you plan your menus and vary the basic recipes as you feel comfortable making them, the fun and the challenge begins, the drudgery ends.

It is easy to imagine the presentation of food as an art form. Think of all the paintings of food, the provocative pages of food advertisements, alive with dewy berries, steaming casseroles, icy glasses of champagne! All the colors of the rainbow are at your disposal, ready to be used. Aside from the nutritional values, the color of food stimulates appetites and freshens palates.

Contrast a delicately browned roast chicken with the fresh green of new peas, the deep red of pickled beets, the pinkish glow of small new potatoes cooked in their skins. For dessert, a deep burgundy-colored boysenberry sherbet can be used as counterpoint to mandarin orange segments, topped with slivered almonds for color, texture, and contrast.

At the other end of the color scale, use your sense of fantasy and create a single-colored meal. I'll never forget the idea of an all white ski picnic in the snow. The skiers carrying backpacks of hot vichyssoise, endive and raw mushroom salad, chicken breasts rolled with ham, coconut cake, and half bottles of Chablis. Very otherworldly and exotic but, with a little preparation, certainly possible. Try doing something for the drama of the color alone. Canned black bean soup is quite respectable—especially if it has a healthy shot of sherry and some chopped egg and a lemon slice added. Served in glass or colorful porcelain bowls, it will lift the soup course out of the realm of the ordinary.

The attraction of the different aromas of food may seem obvious, but why not take advantage of them? In Middle Eastern cuisine, rose and orange flower water are often used for the delicate aroma they impart.

I know of a real estate agent who always tells her clients that the way to get the house sold for the highest price is to show it only between 4:00 and 7:00 P.M. with a turkey baking in the oven and the table set for company. They use up a few turkeys (fed to the family anyway) but they always get the highest prices for their property!

Taste and smell are so intertwined that it is impossible to delineate where one ends and the other begins. Cloves and ginger work their spells as much with fragrance as with taste, as do vanilla, curry, saffron, and many other herbs and spices. Baking intensifies both flavors and aromas, perfuming the air as the food is being prepared.

Texture is more subtle, perhaps, but equally important. The crunchy texture of salad greens served with a smooth entrée is one of the first things that comes to mind. Chinese chefs are masters at working these textural and visual surprises. The slightly sweet, mild flavor of crisp water chestnuts adds a fine contrast to stir-fried foods; the proportion, color, and slight difference in texture between their slippery tree mushrooms, delicate snow pea pods, almonds, walnuts, and pecans tell the story of texture perfectly.

Try using poppy seeds on buttered egg noodles to add interest and variety. Sesame seeds sprinkled on rolled filets of sole add a textural interest to a delicate, easy to prepare dish (see pages 180–181).

There are no hard and fast rules in preparing food. The traditions aren't really limitations at all, because there are so many to choose from. Hot and cold, sweet and sour, bland and spicy—they are all present in one cuisine or another. Think of the bravery of the first person who ate a raw oyster or an egg! Take a deep breath, follow your instincts and experiment.

5
Herbs and Spices

Since many foods are enhanced by the judicious use of herbs and spices, you may want to know a little more about them. A small amount of a spice can make an ordinary dish sing with flavor and fragrance. The line between herbs and spices becomes fuzzy at times but, in general, herbs are flavorful plant leaves, such as parsley, dill, thyme, chives, tarragon. Usually green when fresh, they are used in both fresh and dried forms. Spices are usually the stronger, more pungent and aromatic, flavoring aids—like cloves, cinnamon, nutmeg, allspice, and, of course, the various kinds of pepper. Most often (though not always) dried, some spices are seeds or seedpods, some come from the bark of woody plants, and still others, like ginger, are roots. To complicate matters further, there are seeds of herbs and other plants—poppy, caraway, dill, anise, sesame—that are used and treated like dried herbs and spices.

There are several good rules to remember regarding seasonings. The importance of keeping herbs and spices in tightly closed containers, away from light, cannot be emphasized enough. You must use them as quickly as possible, so buy the smallest quantity you can. Try not to keep them (herbs, especially) for more than four to six months. Take a periodic inventory of your spices, and throw the tired and faded ones out.

Stick to the recipe the first time around, using herbs and spices in the amounts recommended; you can usually add more later. Once you feel confident making a particular dish, you may want to vary it by adding a pinch of a different spice or herb. Whatever you choose, smell it first: Chances are, if it is very pungent or aromatic, it should be used sparingly.

HERBS AND SPICES

Use fresh herbs if you can find them. It is worth the trouble. When you have fresh herbs and they begin to fade, you can dry them yourself by hanging them upside down in a bundle in a well-ventilated area. Then crumble the leaves from the stems and store in a tightly closed glass jar until ready to use. Also remember that dried herbs are generally stronger than fresh: The usual ratio is half the amount of dried herbs to fresh ones. You can substitute one for the other in most recipes—just keep this ratio in mind.

Heating, whether on top of or inside the stove, usually intensifies flavors, so be sure to wait before adding more seasonings. Curry powder, for example, mellows as it cooks, and the flavor becomes much more pronounced. (It also intensifies as it stands in a mayonnaise dressing, so be sure to measure carefully.)

Keep an eye on measurements when using tarragon and oregano as well. They are very strong, and dried tarragon, especially, can overpower a delicately flavored dish (though it is a delicious addition when used wisely). The same holds true for bay leaves.

Here is a brief rundown on some of the more common uses for herbs and spices. The list is by no means complete or absolute, so feel free to experiment.

SEASONING	MOST COMMON USES	FORM AVAILABLE
Allspice (spice)	Meat stews and soups, cakes, cookies, breads	Dried: whole, ground
Anise seed	Licorice-flavored; use in pastry, cookies, some Oriental dishes	Dried: whole, ground
Basil (herb)	Best with tomato sauces, especially Italian dishes	Fresh Dried

SEASONING	MOST COMMON USES	FORM AVAILABLE
Bay leaf (herb)	Leaves of the bay laurel shrub; use sparingly in stews, soups	Dried: whole leaves crushed
Capers (herb)	Seafood, eggs, salads, steak tartare, dishes that use anchovies	Pickled
Caraway seed	Cabbage, sauerkraut, rye bread	Dried
Celery seed	In Bloody Marys, salads, soups	Dried
Chervil (herb)	Delicate flavor; with eggs, seafood, green salads, pot roasts, and stews	Fresh Dried
Chives (herb)	Delicate, onionlike flavor; for fish and seafood, eggs, cream cheese	Fresh Freeze-dried
Cinnamon (spice)	Desserts, fruits, beverages; some Near Eastern and Russian entrées	Dried: stick, ground
Cloves (spice)	Very pungent; use with baked ham; sparingly in soups, cakes; cooked fruits, preserves, hot drinks	Dried: whole, ground
Cumin seed	Strong; use in chili, curry, egg dishes, Mexican dishes, breads; with meats	Dried: whole, ground

HERBS AND SPICES

SEASONING	MOST COMMON USES	FORM AVAILABLE
Dill (seed)	With cabbage, pickles, lamb, salads	Dried
Dill weed (herb)	Delicate, best when fresh; great in sour cream, eggs, seafood dishes, salads	Fresh Dried
Fennel (herb)	Use fresh leaves for a licorice taste in salads; use dried seeds in pastries, cakes	Fresh leaves Dried: whole seeds
Garlic (bulb)	Universal pungent seasoning, cooked or raw	Fresh, juice, or Dried: minced, ground
Ginger (spice)	Oriental dishes, curries, stewed fruit desserts, gingerbread; in crystallized form, as candy or topping	Fresh root Dried: ground, cracked, crystallized
Horseradish (herb)	Adds pep to salad dressings, dips, roast beef sauces	Fresh root Prepared
Marjoram (herb)	Mild; good with veal, lamb, poultry, stuffings, eggs	Fresh Dried
Mint (herb)	In jellies, sauces for lamb; as garnish for salads, desserts, drinks	Fresh Dried
Mustard (seed)	Tangy; in pickles, cabbage dishes; also wide range of other uses	Dried: ground Prepared

SEASONING	MOST COMMON USES	FORM AVAILABLE
Nutmeg (spice)	All-purpose aromatic; with meats, on spinach, many vegetables, in sauces, beverages, desserts	Dried: whole, ground
Oregano (herb)	Many Italian dishes, pizza, salad, tomato dishes	Fresh Dried
Paprika (spice)	Made from sweet red peppers; universal use; important ingredient in Hungarian poultry and meat dishes; mild all-purpose garnish for fish, poultry, vegetables	Dried: ground
Parsley (herb)	Universal garnish; with eggs, soups, poultry, meat, salads, vegetables	Fresh Dried
Pepper: black, white, green, (spice)	The true pepper; universal seasoning; black pepper includes outer hull or peppercorn; white pepper has outer hull removed and is good for creamy sauces, seafood, fish; green	Dried: whole, ground

HERBS AND SPICES

SEASONING	MOST COMMON USES	FORM AVAILABLE
	pepper is unripe whole peppercorn, used for milder flavor	
Pepper: hot (Capsicum)	These are the New World peppers: cayenne, chili, green, jalapeño, and others; also the Indian, Chinese, and Szechwan; a touch adds zest; use sparingly. Its juice can irritate skin, so wear rubber gloves, do not rub eyes when preparing fresh hot peppers.	Fresh Dried: crushed, ground Pickled
Poppy seed	With noodles; in and on breads, rolls, cakes, cookies	Dried
Rosemary (herb)	Aromatic; good with lamb, veal, pork	Dried
Saffron (spice)	The stigma of a variety of crocus; expensive; mild flavor; used extensively in Spanish and Indian cooking; use to add golden color, aroma, to breads, rice, seafood sauces	Dried

SEASONING	MOST COMMON USES	FORM AVAILABLE
Sage (herb)	Eggs, cheese, poultry stuffing, salads, most vegetables	Fresh Dried: whole, ground
Savory (herb)	The summer and winter varieties are similar in flavor; use with eggs, salad, cheese, chicken, hamburger, sauces, stuffings	Fresh Dried
Sesame seed	Mild, nutty flavor; adds crunch texture to salads, breads and rolls, entrées, desserts	Dried
Shallots (bulb)	Elegant cousin of the onion; delicate flavor; use anywhere onions are used	Fresh Freeze-dried
Tarragon (herb)	Pungent; use sparingly in eggs, seafood, salads, tomato dishes; for flavoring vinegar	Fresh Dried: whole, ground
Thyme (herb)	Basic seasoning in French and Continental cooking; fragrant and useful everywhere	Fresh Dried: whole, ground
Vanilla	The seedpod (bean) of a Central American orchid; used in desserts, on fruit	Dried: whole Extract

HERBS AND SPICES 67

As you experiment with different herbs and spices, you will probably come to have your own particular favorites, the ones you rely on to add your own "secret" touch. These are a few that I think deserve special attention, along with a few notes on some frequently used combinations of herbs and spices. These mixtures—like curry powder, fines herbes and others—occur in a number of recipes in this book, and other cookbooks call for similar concoctions. Most are available in packaged form, but in some cases you may want to make your own. Since they combine different ingredients, you are at liberty to adjust the proportions to make your own favorite herb or spice the "high" note of your version.

BOUQUET GARNI

This combination of parsley, thyme, and bay leaf is frequently used in chicken and beef soups and stews. It can be used to add flavor to almost any dish that needs to cook for a long time. It is available in dried form to sprinkle directly into the pot, but if possible, be a purist and tie the ingredients in a cheesecloth bag. Use 4 sprigs of parsley, a branch of fresh thyme (if you can find it—if not, use about 1 teaspoon dried thyme), and a bay leaf; add a leek and a few stalks of celery, leaves and all. Wrap everything up in cheesecloth and tie with cotton thread or string; when the soup or stew is done, you can remove the herbs easily.

CAPERS

These tiny Mediterranean buds can be found in most supermarkets, pickled in a vinegary brine. (The smaller they are, the better.) Try them along with chopped onions and chopped eggs as an accompaniment to smoked salmon. They are also a fine garnish for broiled fish of all kinds and are one of the requirements for Steak Tartare (pages 134–135). They need no refrigeration and keep almost indefinitely.

CHILI POWDER

This premixed prerequisite for Tex-Mex specialties is a blend of ground chili peppers, cumin, oregano, garlic, salt, and sometimes other ingredients, such as allspice or cloves. It can be a "secret ingredient" for snapping up a bland sauce.

CURRY POWDER

Curry powder, which we buy here as a single spice, is actually a blend of many spices mixed in different proportions and strengths by each manufacturer. In India, Pakistan, and certain provinces of China, there are as many curry concoctions as there are cooks. It is usually a mixture of various combinations and amounts of ginger, cayenne pepper, red pepper, black pepper, cloves, nutmeg, cinnamon, cumin, mustard seed, turmeric, coriander, fenugreek, cardamom, and paprika!

For obvious reasons, unless you are a real connoisseur of Indian food, you may as well buy a prepared curry powder. They vary in intensity and "high" notes and, if you are fond of curries (and there are countless variations and recipes) you can experiment with different brands until you find a favorite. Gourmet shops often carry curry pastes as well as powders (to be used in the same way), and some import Indian curry—usually quite pungent—that can be purchased in bulk form by the ounce or pound. Among the American brands, Spice Islands and Crosse & Blackwell are quite good. Like all aromatics, buy only what can be used within a couple months at the most.

DILL WEED

The sleeping giant of the herb garden, dill is best when fresh; it is easy to find during the summer, and better groceries carry it all year round. If you have a garden, the very name, dill *weed,* should give you some idea of how easy it is to grow. So delicate in flavor that it is almost impossible to use too much, it is a fine addition to salads, eggs, cheese dishes, fish, and breads. The seeds are used in making relishes and pickles; and the lacy leaves of the weed, fresh or dried, are almost the textbook companion for cucumbers. With a dilled homemade mayonnaise, a cold lobster becomes legendary. Cold poached salmon with fresh dill is another beautiful dish—both to look at and to taste. Dill's natural affinity for sour cream has made it a basic herb in Russian and Slavic cooking. Try sprinkling vichyssoise (potato soup) with chopped dill and fresh black pepper instead of the traditional chopped chives (or use both). It is also wonderful tossed with buttered string beans or small boiled potatoes.

FINES HERBES

A combination of chervil, tarragon, parsley, chives, sometimes also basil or sage, fines herbes is most frequently used in French recipes. It is a distinctive addition to salads and egg dishes as well, and will add a special touch to most Continental dishes.

Fines herbes can be found in most supermarkets, but you can make it yourself very easily; simply combine 1 tablespoon each of dried tarragon, dried parsley, dried chervil, and freeze-dried chives. If you wish to use any of the ingredients in its fresh form, double the amount. (Unless you have an herb garden, however, it is unlikely that you will run across fresh chervil. If you can't find chervil at all, double the parsley and hope for the best.) Always make these herb combinations in small batches so they will stay fresh and aromatic.

HERBES DE PROVENCE

Every cook has his own trade secret. For me, it's the combination of herbs known as herbes de Provence. I throw it into almost everything that would ordinarily call for thyme or oregano, and it seems to do the job with a more subtle and flavorful effect. Available in many gourmet shops, there are a thousand varieties—just like curry powders—and if you decide to make your own, feel free to try your luck at changing the proportions. You can leave out or add one or another ingredient and make it your own special "herbes de Mary Lou," or "herbes de Charlie." Use dried herbs, if possible in whole-leaf form rather than ground—expect for the bay leaf, which should be crumbled as fine as the other herbs for even distribution. The ingredients are given in proportions, not in amounts, so you can make as much or as little as you wish.

3 parts each: thyme, marjoram, chervil (or dried parsley)
2 parts tarragon
1 part each: oregano, rosemary, summer savory
1 bay leaf, crumbled

Combine all the herbs and shake the container vigorously to make sure they are evenly distributed. Store tightly closed.

NUTMEG

Most people think of nutmeg only in terms of desserts, but a sprinkling of freshly grated nutmeg on fresh cabbage, green beans, or cauliflower will transform a nice vegetable into a memorable dish. Also try a bit of it in beef stews. The wonderful aroma of nutmeg has been prized for hundreds of years, and in the eighteenth century dandies used to carry a nutmeg in a pocket case, scraping off a bit to sniff like snuff! (Mace, used in baking, is the dried outer covering of nutmeg.)

POULTRY SEASONING

This combination of sage, powdered onion, marjoram, and thyme is an easy addition to stuffing for fowl. It can also be sprinkled on a roasting bird, although it should be used very sparingly.

SESAME SEED, POPPY SEED

The delicate flavor and texture of sesame and poppy seed make them ideal for an unusual finishing touch on buttered noodles, fish, and salads. If you are making bread or rolls from a mix, or if you buy the brown-and-serve kind, glaze the top with beaten egg white and sprinkle with sesame or poppy seed before baking. Sesame seeds are sometimes available already toasted.

THYME

This herb is a basic requirement for any kitchen of distinction. The fine, needle-thin leaves are essential for many French and Italian dishes and can be added to almost any slow-cooking soup, casserole, or stew—be it vegetable, fish, meat, or fowl. It is also one of the basic ingredients of herbes de Provence. Use fresh thyme or the whole dried leaves if you can, since the ground version is dense and does not mix well in cooking.

6
Saucery and Sorcery

Someone once remarked that the French invented sauces to cover the taste of bad meat. Needless to say, that anonymous wit was either jealous or just didn't know how to cook. Spoiled food is beyond redemption, but a tasty sauce, used with a sense of proportion, can work magic with good food. When you consider that a sauce is any fluid or soft dressing used as an accompaniment to food (or so the dictionary dryly tells us), you'll begin to understand the possibilities. When you realize that sauces include ketchup and mustard, as well as classic French and Italian mayonnaise and tomato sauce, the whole idea comes into focus a little more sharply.

The growth of convenience foods has been accompanied by a multitude of prepared sauces and sauce ingredients that make life a lot simpler. Consider the following, most of which are so well known that they need no elaboration:

TOMATO SAUCES

Ketchup: Now available in spicy, smoke-flavored, pineapple, vinegar, and, of course, regular varieties.

Chili sauce: Not really hot as its name would imply, it is a pungent tomato-based sauce which can be used with meat or fish, anywhere you would use ketchup.

Seafood cocktail sauce: Buy it if you want, but it's just as easy to make your own with chili sauce and a little horseradish.

Spaghetti sauce: If you don't want to make your own (pages 192–193), there are now as many varieties as there are brand names. Take your pick.

SAUCERY AND SORCERY

BARBECUE SAUCES

These are basically either sweet and sour, or hickory-smoke flavored. Ham glaze can also be used for spareribs and other pork products.

STEAK AND GENERAL PURPOSE SAUCES

Escoffier Sauce Robert, Escoffier Sauce Diable: The first is mild; the second, pungent. Both are good on red meats at the table or as a marinade.

A.1. sauce, 57 sauce, Worcestershire sauce: These tangy preparations can be used in salad dressings; to marinate and flavor chicken, game, and vegetables. Worcestershire, especially, should be part of your basic kitchen. Like most of these sauces, it needs no refrigeration and keeps almost indefinitely.

Soy sauce: Once considered exotic, this Oriental flavoring is now widely used in non-Oriental cooking. Surprisingly good in sautéed zucchini or summer squash, on broiling chicken and steaks, with diced leftover meats and rice.

Oriental sauce: A popular soy-based marinade made with wine and spices, you can buy a number of prepared versions (teriyaki sauce, for one), or make it very easily yourself (pages 85–86). Kikkoman from Japan makes a good soy sauce and teriyaki sauce, available in many supermarkets.

PEPPER SAUCES

Tabasco sauce, Jamaican sherry pepper sauce, Mexican jalapeño sauce: To perk up egg and cheese dishes, for Mexican and Spanish dishes, as well as Szechwan and Hunan-style Chinese cooking. A little goes a long way.

MAYONNAISE

The basic ingredient for an enormous variety of sauces. You can buy the commercial variety, but homemade blender mayonnaise (pages 78–79) is so much better. Remember: It does require refrigeration.

PREPARED MUSTARD

Preparations made from the simple mustard seed range through every nuance of flavor, from very mild to the English and Chinese varieties, which are strong enough to bring tears to the eyes. Try a few:

Salad mustard: The mild, bright yellow, hot dog mustard that kids like.

German, or Düsseldorf, mustard: The brownish, mellow mustard, with or without horseradish. This is good with pork and smoked meats and comes as strong or as mild as you wish.

French, or Dijon, mustard: There are dozens of different kinds of mustards available in France, some of which are now available in America. In better supermarkets, you can at least find the imported Dijon mustard, or Dijon-style Grey Poupon, which is made domestically from a French recipe that features white wine. It is a good general mustard for making salad dressings, sauces, and for spreading on broiling steaks and hamburgers.

English and Chinese mustards: These are quite different, but the effect is the same—strong! The English (Coleman's is the most popular here) comes in dry ground and prepared forms. The dry is easiest to use in salad dressings and in cooking. Use sparingly. If you can't find Chinese mustard when called for in a recipe, use Coleman's.

CONDIMENTS AND EXOTIC SAUCES

Chutney: This Indian condiment is a sweet-and-sour chunky sauce served with curries. It is equally good with anything bland that can use the bite of its tangy flavor. The most popular kind here is Major Grey's, not a brand, but a type of chutney made with mangoes, currants or raisins, vinegar and spices. There are also lemon pickle chutneys, harder to find but worth investigating.

Pickle relishes: Dozens of combinations are available. The classic topping for hot dogs and hamburgers.

Also worth considering: Pickled watermelon rind, cantaloupe, pineapple, crabapples, and pears—and, of course, cranberry sauce.

SALAD DRESSINGS

Naturally, you need not be reminded that there are an enormous number of commercially prepared salad dressings. Before resorting to them, try creating one yourself. Creamy Blue Cheese Dressing (page 77) and Russian Dressing (page 80) are always popular. The universal salad dressing, as well as basting sauce, is still the Classic French Vinaigrette (page 76).

SWEET SAUCES

Honey, chocolate sauce, maple syrup, molasses, and various concentrated fruit syrups have a variety of uses, not only in desserts.

BASIC SAUCE INGREDIENTS

Vinegar: Use plain white vinegar for pickling. Wine vinegar is a must for salad dressings. A delicious (and costly) Spanish sherry vinegar is available in a few gourmet shops. Cider vinegar has an interesting tartness. Tarragon and other flavored vinegars are also available, but are worth making yourself (see below).

Oil: Olive, peanut, corn, safflower, as well as the more exotic walnut oil and sesame oil for authentic Oriental cooking.

Wine: If possible, try to cook with the same wine you will serve. If you wouldn't drink it, don't cook with it!

Reconstituted lemon and lime juice: All-purpose cooking aids with many uses—in drinks, cooking, marinades, salad dressing, and on fresh fruit. Can be substituted for vinegar (or half and half) in many recipes. In addition to the reconstituted form, Minute Maid full-strength frozen lemon juice is now available, and it is noticably better.

FLAVORED VINEGARS

With no trouble at all, you can add an extra touch to ever-useful vinegar. Package them yourself in attractive old-fashioned apothecary bottles and give them as gifts. The same variations can be made with cooking sherry or wine as well, used in the same manner.

Pepper vinegar: This will do about the same thing as Tabasco sauce. Cut a cup of fresh hot peppers lengthwise and pour boiling white or cider vinegar over them. Transfer to a bottle and let cool. Keep in the refrigerator. Since vinegar is a preservative, you can keep this almost indefinitely.

You might want to wear rubber gloves as you work—the juice of hot peppers is very irritating.

Tarragon vinegar: Push rinsed fresh tarragon (stems and leaves) into a bottle of cider vinegar. Age for two weeks before using.

Garlic vinegar: This can be used almost everywhere you use vinegar. Start with a good red wine vinegar and slice or crush the garlic (3 or 4 cloves to a pint of vinegar) into the bottle. This ages well, but will be ready to use almost immediately.

Shallot or chive vinegar: For a delicately flavored vinegar, thread fresh shallots, sliced lengthwise, or whole fresh chives into a bottle of wine vinegar. Combine shallots and chives, if you wish. Since these flavors are subtle, age the vinegar for at least two weeks before using.

CLASSIC FRENCH VINAIGRETTE DRESSING

Not to be confused with the nasty bottled orange stuff you get at the supermarket. This absolutely basic French vinaigrette sauce can be used as a salad dressing, as a marinade or basting liquid for chicken, steak, and fish, as a sauce on asparagus or broccoli. Use a high-quality French or Italian olive oil—it makes a difference. Since it is so simple, make it fresh as often as possible. Soon you'll be able to do it almost automatically—it is the same dressing that is served in every fancy French restaurant in the world.

¼ cup wine vinegar
½ to 1 teaspoon Dijon mustard (if you can't find it, use dry mustard)
Salt and freshly ground black pepper to taste
¾ cup olive oil

SAUCERY AND SORCERY

Put the vinegar, mustard, salt, and pepper into a bowl and stir briskly until the salt is dissolved. Add the oil and stir again. (*Hint:* A few drops of water will help keep it homogenized.)

Makes about 1 cup. (If you need less, use the same proportion of 3 parts oil to 1 part vinegar.) As you become experienced you should make it in the bottom of the salad bowl, fresh for each salad.

Variations

For green salads, add a dash of tarragon, dill, chives, mint leaves, or a chopped hard-cooked egg.

With tomatoes, try a dash of basil, oregano, or marjoram.

With cucumbers, use a dash of dill or dill seed, or caraway seed.

With cabbage, try adding 1 teaspoon honey and 1 teaspoon dill seed.

Substitute lemon or lime juice for vinegar.

Rub the salad bowl with bruised garlic before tossing.

SOUR CREAM BLUE CHEESE DRESSING

This is simple to make, fattening as all get-out, and keeps well in the refrigerator. It is a great salad dressing, and can also be used with chopped chives on a baked potato, as a dip for raw vegetables or chips.

1 pint sour cream
¼ to ⅓ pound Blue, Roquefort or Gorgonzola cheese
Juice of ½ lemon
1 teaspoon Worcestershire sauce
Dash of red pepper sauce or cayenne pepper
1 clove garlic, minced (optional)

Break up the cheese with a fork and mix into the sour cream. Don't mix it too thoroughly—the lumps are half the fun. Add the rest of the ingredients, stir well, and return to the refrigerator until ready to use.

Makes about 2½ cups.

Mayonnaise and Mayonnaise-Based Sauces

Mayonnaise is not only one of the most popular sauces, it is the basis of an entire repertoire of classic sauces. You can make your own mayonnaise easily with a blender. There is all the difference in the world between the taste of homemade mayonnaise and even the best of the commercial kinds. The simple addition of an extra ingredient or two can make dozens of delicious creamy sauces: watercress, garlic, lemon peel, curry powder, horseradish, chutney, dill—in fact, almost any savory herb, spice, or condiment you would use with fish, meat, or vegetables. If you can't make your own from scratch, add finely chopped ingredients to the commercial variety before serving. Remember that all mayonnaise must be refrigerated if not used soon after making.

BASIC BLENDER MAYONNAISE

Beating mayonnaise by hand is a chore, but if you have a blender it is child's play. The oil you use is up to you: corn or peanut oil makes a lighter-tasting mayonnaise; olive oil is a heavier, richer oil and makes a more luxurious mayonnaise; or, you can combine different oils. White pepper or pepper sauce is suggested because the speckles of black pepper would be more conspicuous in the sauce. (Of course, if you use black pepper, everyone will know you made it by yourself!)

> 1 large egg
> ½ teaspoon dry mustard or Dijon mustard
> ½ teaspoon salt
> Dash of white pepper or pepper sauce
> 2 tablespoons lemon juice or vinegar
> 1 cup salad or olive oil

Put the egg, mustard, salt, pepper, and lemon juice in a blender. Pour in ¼ cup of the oil, cover, and turn the blender on to a low or "homogenize" speed. Uncover immediately and pour in the remaining oil in a slow, steady stream. When all the oil has been added, switch the blender speed to high for a few seconds and

SAUCERY AND SORCERY 79

then switch it off. It should thicken quite quickly and, with a little practice, you will become adept at it. Store covered in the refrigerator.

Makes about 1¼ cups.

Variations

The following recipes for flavored mayonnaises will make approximately 1 to 1¼ cups of sauce which will be ample for most uses.

CURRIED MAYONNAISE: Great with cold meats and fish, or in tuna salad.

Combine 1 cup mayonnaise, 1 or 2 tablespoons prepared curry powder, and 1 teaspoon lemon juice. Mix together with a fork until well blended. Refrigerate for an hour or so before using. (The curry will "bloom"—develop its flavor—as it stands, so if it tastes a little too bland at first, wait for half an hour or so before adding more curry.)

GARLIC MAYONNAISE: For a perky Mediterranean flavor with hot or cold fish, or bland vegetables.

Combine 1 cup mayonnaise, 3 to 4 cloves garlic (finely minced or crushed), and a dash of cayenne pepper. Be sure the garlic is finely minced or put through a garlic press, or there will be little "explosions" of garlic in the sauce. Mix well and serve cold or at room temperature.

HERBED MAYONNAISE: Excellent on cold meats, fish and poultry.

To 1 cup mayonnaise, add up to ¼ cup chopped fresh herbs—one or more as the spirit moves you—and mix thoroughly. Try parsley, basil, tarragon, chives, or even mint. Chopped fresh dill, all by itself, makes an elegant sauce for cold poached (or canned) salmon.

WATERCRESS MAYONNAISE: This one has a lovely pale green color and works wonders with any delicately flavored fish or cold poultry.

Combine 1 cup mayonnaise, 1 teaspoon lemon juice, and ¼ cup minced watercress, and mix together thoroughly. That's all there is to it! This can be done in the blender after making basic mayonnaise.

TARTAR SAUCE: This is the ideal simple sauce for seafood, especially fried shrimp and broiled fresh fish.

Combine 1 cup mayonnaise, 2 tablespoons each of pickle relish and capers, 1 teaspoon Dijon mustard, 1 tablespoon wine vinegar or lemon juice, and ¼ teaspoon sugar. Mix well and refrigerate for 3 to 4 hours.

EASY RUSSIAN (OR THOUSAND ISLAND) DRESSING: Simple to make and easy to keep, it is a popular salad dressing and dip for raw vegetables. It also can be used to make very respectable eggs à la Russe, which really are only hard-cooked eggs garnished with a spoonful of Russian dressing.

Combine 1 cup mayonnaise, ¼ cup chili sauce or ketchup, 3 tablespoons pickle or green tomato relish, and 1 teaspoon prepared horseradish. You can also add 1 tablespoon of finely chopped raw onion, if you wish. Mix together thoroughly and keep refrigerated.

Makes approximately 1½ cups.

HORSERADISH CREAM SAUCE: A delicious sauce for cold roast beef and ham, or other cold meats. Freshly grated horseradish can be used, as well as either the red or white prepared varieties (the red horseradish prepared with beet juice makes a nice pink sauce).

Beat ½ cup heavy cream into ½ cup mayonnaise until smooth. Add 2 to 3 tablespoons horseradish, juice of ½ lemon, and a dash of hot pepper sauce or pinch of cayenne pepper. Stir until well blended and refrigerate for one hour or more to allow the sauce to thicken.

Makes approximately 1¼ cups.

HORSERADISH MAYONNAISE: If you are in a hurry, this is a simpler version of the horseradish cream sauce. Simply omit the heavy cream and use 1 cup of mayonnaise, combining it with the remaining ingredients as directed.

MOCK HOLLANDAISE SAUCE: Real food snobs turn up their noses at this sort of thing, but where convenience is all important, try this easy-to-make version. It is a useful and flavorful sauce for broccoli, asparagus, cauliflower, or any plain boiled or steamed vegetables.

Melt ¼ cup butter or margarine over low heat. Beat in 1½ tablespoons lemon juice, and 1½ cups mayonnaise, using a whisk or egg beater. Then heat very slowly, beating continuously, for about 2 minutes. Add a few drops of red pepper sauce, if you wish.

Serve warm.

Makes approximately 2 cups.

Béchamel and Other White Sauces

This family of cooked sauces is the base for innumerable dishes, from humble creamed chipped beef and chicken à la king (of nostalgic memory from school and military service days) and almost everything creamed, to all those delicious crumb or cheese-topped au gratin creations of French haute cuisine.

BÉCHAMEL SAUCE
(Basic White Sauce)

Don't let the fancy French name put you off. This classic sauce is the basis of the entire group of white sauces. It's really very simple, and once you get the hang of it, you'll be turning it out with the best of them.

- 3 tablespoons butter or margarine
- 3 tablespoons flour
- 1¾ to 2 cups milk
- Salt and pepper to taste

Melt the butter slowly in a heavy pan over moderate heat. Add the flour as soon as the butter is melted. (In this sauce, you do not want the butter to brown). Stir vigorously with a wooden spoon, rubbing out any lumps, and cook for 2 to 3 minutes until the mixture turns pale gold. Turn the heat down very low and slowly add the milk, stirring constantly. (You can vary the thickness of the sauce with the amount of milk you use.) When you have stirred in all the milk, turn the heat up to moderate and cook until thickened. Season with salt and pepper to taste.

Makes approximately 2 to 2¼ cups.

MORNAY SAUCE

This versatile white cheese sauce is used on vegetables, fish, poultry, and stuffed crepes.

Simply stir approximately ⅓ cup grated Gruyère or Swiss cheese gradually into the béchamel sauce before removing from the heat, warming it just long enough (over moderate heat) to melt the cheese.

SOUBISE SAUCE

A fragrant onion sauce, this can be truly distinctive with any delicately flavored fish or poultry, and as the basic sauce for a casserole of your own creation—for instance, mixed with cooked chicken, broccoli, and noodles or rice.

Sauté 1 cup finely chopped onions in a little butter until soft and lightly browned. Prepare the basic béchamel sauce and add the sautéed onions, along with ⅔ cup grated Parmesan or Gruyère cheese (or a combination of both). Cook over moderate heat, stirring constantly, until the cheese has melted and the flavors are blended.

Serve warm.

BASIC VELOUTÉ SAUCE

This is excellent on poached or broiled fish, poultry or delicate meats. Use fish stock (court bouillon, page 179), chicken stock (page 100), or beef stock (page 100), depending on the type of dish you are serving.

To make it, simply prepare the basic béchamel sauce, except substitute fish, chicken, or beef stock for the milk. If you want a creamier sauce, use half milk and half stock.

TARRAGON VELOUTÉ

This is particularly good on salmon, haddock, halibut, and swordfish steaks.

Prepare the basic béchamel sauce, adding ¼ teaspoon dry (or ½ teaspoon fresh chopped) tarragon to the melted butter before stirring in the flour, and substituting fish stock (court bouillon, page 179) for the milk.

SUPER-RICH WHITE SAUCE

Prepare the basic béchamel sauce, substituting heavy cream or half-and-half for the milk. When serving on vegetables, grate fresh nutmeg on top immediately before serving.

Other White Sauce Variations

Add 2 to 4 tablespoons minced fresh parsley or watercress to the basic béchamel sauce, and heat very gently for 3 minutes.

Add sautéed mushrooms, sliced or minced, to the basic béchamel sauce and heat thoroughly.

BROWN SAUCE

A versatile French sauce used for a variety of roasted meat dishes. It can be made in advance, stored in a jar, and kept cool for later use.

To make it, melt 6 tablespoons butter in a small saucepan and when it turns light brown, add 5 tablespoons flour, stirring until smooth. Then gradually add 1½ cups hot bouillon (canned or made from cubes), stirring constantly until blended. Season with salt and pepper to taste, and simmer slowly for 20 minutes. If the sauce gets too thick, add more bouillon.

PAN GRAVY FOR MEAT AND CHICKEN

This can be prepared while your roasted meat or poultry is "setting" (resting for a few minutes to set the flavor and make it easier to carve). You can even do it in the bottom of your roasting pan, set on a burner of the stove.

Heat ¼ cup of the pan drippings in a saucepan and slowly add ¼ cup flour. Brown, stirring constantly, for about 3 minutes over medium heat. Turn off the heat. With a wooden spoon, stir 2 cups of stock or bouillon around in the roasting pan, loosening any browned bits left in the pan. (Heat gently if necessary.) Add this liquid to the flour mixture in the saucepan and cook over medium heat, stirring constantly, until it thickens. Then simmer for 5 minutes. Season with salt and pepper to taste.

RÉMOULADE SAUCE

This is the very classy sauce that French restaurants often serve on cold mussels, shrimp, and fish. It is also good on cold cooked vegetables and crudités (page 93).

Combine 1 teaspoon well-drained pickle relish, 1 tablespoon Dijon mustard, 2 chopped hard-cooked egg yolks, and a sprinkling of salt and pepper. Mix lightly with a fork. Dribble in 1 cup olive oil very slowly, while mixing briskly. Allow to stand for a few minutes to meld the flavors.

LEMON AND BUTTER SAUCE

A simple basting sauce while broiling fish. It is also good poured on cooked fish and vegetables before serving.

Melt 4 tablespoons butter slowly in a small pan. Stir in the juice of ½ lemon and a dash of cayenne pepper. Pour or dab on with a pastry brush.

Marinades

For centuries, cooks have known the benefits of using sauces (called marinades) that tenderize and add flavor to meats and fish. Game meats, like venison and wild fowl, are particularly enhanced by marinades, which help to minimize their "gamy" taste as well as their toughness.

A wide variety of sauces, both commercial and homemade, can be used as quick marinades. Commercial meat tenderizer or lemon pepper from your supermarket spice rack can be used as a marinade, either alone or with other ingredients. The classic French vinaigrette dressing (page 76) and Oriental sauce (below) can also be used to marinate meat.

Since many marinades contain acidic ingredients (like wine, vinegar, or lemon juice), it is best to use a plastic, glass, or ceramic dish for soaking the meat. Cooked marinades should be allowed to cool before being used. Remember, also, that temperature affects the timing. If you have time, the refrigerator is the proper place to marinate meats and, especially, fish. If this is not possible, keep the bowl covered and in a cool spot.

Turn meats periodically to ensure even penetration of the sauce. When using chunks of meat (for kebobs or stews), put a plate on top and weight it down with something heavy to keep the meat submerged in the marinade; or use a plastic bag, sealed tightly, for your marinating, turning from time to time to keep the process going. Use extra sauce for basting the meat as it cooks.

ORIENTAL SAUCE

Japanese and Chinese cooking is becoming increasingly popular throughout the United States. Here's one easy way to get on the Orient Express. This soy-based sauce can be used to marinate steak, chicken, pork chops, and lamb. It also can be splashed on sliced zucchini while it's cooking in a frying pan or wok.

½ cup soy sauce
¼ cup dry sherry or white wine
1 clove garlic, minced, or 5 to 6 drops garlic juice
1 teaspoon freshly grated ginger, or ½ teaspoon ground ginger
1 tablespoon honey
1 tablespoon peanut, sesame or other light salad oil.

Combine all the ingredients in a bowl, and stir well. Transfer to a plastic bottle, capping tightly. If possible, keep refrigerated until ready to use. Shake briskly before using.

GARLIC MARINADE FOR MEAT AND FISH

⅔ cup wine vinegar or leftover red wine
⅔ cup olive or peanut oil
3 cloves garlic, chopped
1 teaspoon thyme or fines herbes
½ teaspoon coarsely ground black pepper
1 teaspoon salt

Combine all ingredients and stir well. Pour over meat or fish. Allow to marinate overnight in the refrigerator, or 2 to 3 hours at room temperature. Baste the meat with extra marinade as it roasts or broils.

LEMON MARINADE FOR FISH AND CHICKEN

¾ cup lemon juice
¼ cup salad oil
2 tablespoons finely chopped fresh parsley
2 tablespoons chopped shallots or the white part of scallions (reserve green scallion tops)
½ teaspoon salt
¼ teaspoon freshly ground pepper

Soak the chicken or fish in the marinade for several hours. Baste with the sauce when cooking (broiling or baking). Chop the tops of the scallions into tiny bits and add 5 minutes before serving. (Their delicate flavor would be lost if you added them earlier.)

COOKED WINE MARINADE FOR VENISON AND OTHER GAME

This is also good for marinating steak.

- 2½ cups dry red wine
- 1 carrot, cut into small pieces
- 1 onion, coarsely chopped
- 1 bay leaf
- 1 teaspoon thyme
- ½ teaspoon salt
- ½ teaspoon coarsely ground black pepper

Combine all the ingredients in a saucepan and simmer gently for 30 minutes. Allow to cool before using.

CRANBERRY SAUCE

This is so easy to make at home, it is silly to buy it.

- 1 pound fresh cranberries
- 2 cups sugar
- 1 cup water

Put the ingredients into a saucepan and heat to boiling. Boil rapidly until the berries pop open (about 5 minutes), and remove from the heat. Cool in the bowl you will use to serve it. You can keep it, covered, in the refrigerator for at least a week.

CLASSIC ITALIAN TOMATO SAUCE (SEE PAGE 192)

PESTO SAUCE (SEE PAGE 193)

7

Great Beginnings:

Appetizers and Hors d'Oeuvres

The following recipes show the almost limitless ways to begin a meal, as well as add to the enjoyment of a cocktail party. You might want to combine a selection of several for an informal supper or luncheon, since most of them can be prepared in advance, leaving you free to be with your guests. Plain or fancy, they all can be accomplished easily.

PICKLED MUSHROOMS
(Champignons à la Grecque)

Despite the French name, these mushrooms, pickled in the Greek style, couldn't be easier to make. They will keep for several days in the refrigerator.

> 1 pound fresh mushrooms
> 1 cup classic French vinaigrette dressing (page 76)
> ¼ cup chopped fresh parsley

Wipe the raw mushrooms with damp paper towels to remove dirt. (Washing them in water makes them soggy, and you want them to absorb dressing, not water.) Trim the stems and slice the mushrooms uniformly. Toss with the dressing and chopped parsley. Keep cool or refrigerate for a few hours before serving to allow them to marinate.

Serves 4.

ANTIPASTO

If you have a reasonably well stocked delicatessen or gourmet food shop nearby, there is nothing more satisfying as a first course, or as a tray at a party, than the classic Italian antipasto. It can include almost anything, but try to have at least a few of the following delicacies on your platter: sweet roasted peppers (or pimientos) with anchovies, provolone cheese, hard Italian sausage (like Genoa salami), hot Tuscan peppers, black olives, sliced ripe tomatoes, quartered hard-cooked eggs, quartered celery hearts, and marinated artichoke hearts.

If you are lucky enough to have an Italian delicatessen in your area, you also may be able to find the marvelous combination of prosciutto (Italian ham) and Mozzarella cheese, wound together like a jelly roll. It is usually sold by the pound and you can buy as much as you need. Cut the roll crosswise into thin slices, with the pale pink of the ham intersecting the ivory cheese, and spear on toothpicks.

Arrange your choice of ingredients attractively on a serving platter, drizzle some good olive oil and wine vinegar on top, add a sprinkling of coarsely ground pepper fresh from the mill, and serve.

STUFFED FRENCH BREAD

Making the same thing in a slightly different way sometimes makes all the difference. Instead of ordinary sandwiches, for instance, stuff the fixings into a crusty loaf of French or Italian bread. Slice the loaf very thinly and you have appealing hors d'oeuvres. Cut into more generous portions, the stuffed bread becomes hearty sandwiches, great for a festive picnic or a shipboard lunch or supper. Use one of the fillings suggested here or invent your own. Since the bread is to be cut after filling, however, don't concoct anything too thin, gooey or runny. To prepare the bread, cut the loaf crosswise into 4- to 6-inch pieces. Hollow out the center of each piece, removing all but the outer half inch or so of bread and crust, and fill with the desired mixture (packing it in firmly). Wrap in plastic film or aluminum foil and refrigerate for several hours before slicing. For hors d'oeuvres, cut into ½-inch thick slices; for luncheon or supper sandwiches, make the slices at least 1 inch thick. Garnish with chopped parsley, if desired.

Fillings

MEAT AND CHEESE: Roll thin slices of cold cooked meat and cheese "jelly-roll" style and wedge into the cavity of the bread. Use Swiss cheese and ham, salami and Mozzarella, chicken and sharp Cheddar, corned beef and Muenster.

CREAM CHEESE FILLINGS: The cream cheese fillings on page 95 are excellent for stuffing French bread. You will need 1 to 2 recipes, depending on the size of your bread.

TUNA SALAD: Use your own favorite tuna salad recipe, or try a curried tuna salad (page 116). Make it as dry and solid as possible so it won't run out of the bread. Line the cavity of the bread with Boston or other leaf lettuce before stuffing in the tuna salad.

CAPONATA: A savory Italian eggplant and olive appetizer, it is available canned in most groceries and supermarkets. Drain some of the sauce so it won't be too runny, and line the cavity of the bread with leaves of lettuce.

RATATOUILLE: Use cold ratatouille (page 200), wrapped in lettuce, and be sure to drain some of the sauce.

CREAM CHEESE AND CHUTNEY

This sounds revolting, but, believe it or not, it's quite good, unusual, and takes only about a minute to put together. There must have been an actual Major Grey once, but the name now refers to a type of mango chutney. (Crosse & Blackwell brand is good.)

1 package cream cheese (any size)
1 bottle Major Grey's chutney

Simply put the cheese on a plate, allow to reach room temperature, and cover the top with the chutney. Serve with crackers. The two tastes blend surprisingly well together. If you wish, you can combine the cheese and the chutney with a fork, adding a little milk to make it mix more smoothly.

Serve with crackers.

SMOKED SALMON (LOX)

This aristocrat of appetizers is quite expensive, but makes an excellent first act for a memorable meal. It is available freshly sliced in metropolitan area delicatessens and supermarkets and in packages in better food stores elsewhere. Allow ½ pound for 3 people. Serve it the French way on a bed of lettuce with finely chopped raw onions, capers, and/or hard-cooked eggs as a garnish. You can also dribble a little olive oil on each portion and then squeeze a wedge of lemon on top. Since lox is quite salty (more salty than the similar Nova Scotia salmon) it won't need additional salt, but a fine sprinkling of freshly ground pepper is good. Thickly sliced black bread and sweet butter are an ideal accompaniment.

CHOPPED CHICKEN LIVERS (PÂTÉ)

Pâté is simply the French word for paste, and can be applied to almost anything that is puréed. This recipe takes some doing, but the results are worth it. To purée the ingredients, you'll need a blender or, better still, a food mill, which will give a more interesting texture to the pâté. Serve either on toast as canapés, or on a lettuce leaf as a first course.

- ¼ pound bacon
- 1 pound chicken livers
- 2 onions, finely sliced
- 3 tablespoons butter
- 1 teaspoon salt, or to taste
- ¼ teaspoon freshly ground pepper
- ¼ teaspoon thyme
- ¼ teaspoon nutmeg
- 3 tablespoons brandy or cognac
- 2 hard-cooked eggs

Fry the bacon until crisp and drain on paper towels, then crumble into bits and set aside. Wash and dry your frying pan and melt the butter in it. Add the chicken livers and onions and sprinkle the seasonings over them. Cook uncovered, at a moderately high temperature for approximately 5 minutes. Turn off the heat and add the brandy to the hot mixture. Put all the ingredients through a food grinder (or a blender), using a little of each at a time, until well ground and free of lumps. Stir thoroughly and press firmly into an attractive serving dish. Chill for 2 or 3 hours in the refrigerator before serving. Garnish with parsley or fancy cut radishes.

Serves 6 to 8.

SHRIMP WITH DILL

1 pound shrimp or other shellfish (such as crabmeat, lobster)
1 cup classic French vinaigrette dressing (page 76)
⅓ cup chopped fresh dill or to taste

Cook the shrimp for 3 to 5 minutes, depending on size. (If frozen, read directions on the package.) Remove the larger stems before chopping the dill. Allow the shrimp to cool and then toss lightly with the French dressing and the dill. The dill is so fragrant and delicate that you need not fear overdoing it, so use as much as you wish. Chill before serving.

Serves 4.

TARAMA

The tangy Greek fish roe makes an interesting appetizer. (See Salads, pages 109–116).

Simple No-Cook, No-Work Hors d'Oeuvres

Try some of these when you have to whip up an elegant appetizer in a hurry:

Herring tidbits in wine sauce or in sour cream.

Cold cooked shrimp with cocktail sauce, spiked with ½ teaspoon of horseradish.

Smoked oysters or clams, drained and served with lemon wedges on Melba toast rounds.

Crudités (page 93).

Pimientos and anchovies.

Canned clams or mussels in a classic French vinaigrette

dressing (page 76), a rémoulade sauce (page 84), or curried mayonnaise (page 79).

Crabmeat lumps with cocktail sauce or a classic French vinaigrette dressing (page 76).

Canned stuffed grape leaves (available in Greek specialty shops).

Cheddar or Swiss cheese and salami bits skewered on a toothpick.

Chunks of honeydew or Persian melon, wrapped with strips of Italian prosciutto ham or salami and speared with toothpicks.

Thin slices of cold roast beef or smoked ham filled with spoonfuls of herbed cream cheese spread (page 95), rolled into tubes, and fastened with toothpicks. Dip the ends in chopped parsley.

Simple canapés—crackers or small squares and triangles of thin toast or bread, topped with deviled sardines, caviar, or other spread (pages 95–96).

CRUDITÉS

This amusing sounding word does not mean what you might think it does. Anything but crude, it refers to prettily prepared raw vegetables to be served with a sauce or dip for hors d'oeuvres at home, on a boat, or at a picnic. At a cocktail party, they are a godsend for dieters when all there is to munch on with the booze is the usual assortment of rich canapés.

They can be almost anything eaten raw—carrot strips, cauliflower segments, endive sections, radishes, green pepper strips, scallions, celery, cherry tomatoes—anything that looks well together. They are more interesting than fussy hors d'oeuvres, and healthy to boot. Try arranging a tray of whatever vegetables look freshest at the market and serve them as a colorful still life surrounding bowls of one or more of the sauces found on pages 76–81. Curried mayonnaise and blue cheese dressing, for example, are perennial favorites, and you might also want to try watercress or dilled mayonnaise. A few slices of lemon on the tray might also be appreciated by dieters and others who prefer their vegetables straight.

STUFFED RAW VEGETABLES

Fresh raw vegetables, used as "containers" for a variety of fillings, make an unusual hors d'oeuvre. These tidbits require no cooking, just a little time and patience. You can use a variety of vegetables and any number of fillings—in endless combinations. Here are a few tips on vegetables that are appropriate for stuffing and how to prepare them. Stuff with any of the fillings on pages 95–96. Of course, when selecting a filling, you must keep in mind the size of the vegetable you're going to stuff: chunky egg or tuna salad, for example, are better for stuffing large tomatoes than for tiny cherry tomatoes. Don't stop with this list, though—with a little imagination you can devise your own combinations and fillings.

Vegetables for Stuffing

CHERRY OR PLUM TOMATOES: Wash and hollow out inside with a paring knife.

CUCUMBERS: Scrub well, using soap if the skin has been coated with oil or wax. Then cut into 1½-inch chunks and hollow out the center with a teaspoon or melon ball scoop.

RAW MUSHROOMS: Remove the stems and wipe the caps clean with damp paper towels. Use the caps for stuffing and reserve the stems for a soup or stew.

CELERY: Just cut off the leafy tops, wash the stalks well, and pat dry with paper towels. If you wish, you can cut long stalks into several pieces after filling.

ARTICHOKE BOTTOMS: You can't stuff these raw, but you don't have to cook them yourself. Cooked artichoke bottoms, as well as the marinated kind, are available in cans or jars. Simply drain and use the natural depression for your filling, scraping it out a little if necessary.

ZUCCHINI: Prepare in the same way as cucumbers.

Filling and Spreads for Raw Vegetables and Canapés

These are excellent as stuffings and dips for fresh raw vegetables, spreads for canapés, and fillings for tiny pastry puffs and shells.

Cream Cheese Fillings

Cream cheese makes an excellent base for a variety of fillings. Start by combining an 8-ounce package of cream cheese and 2 tablespoons butter softened to room temperature. (If you wish, use whipped cream cheese, which is a little more manageable.) If you are making a dip, thin the mixture with a little milk, then blend in any of the following:

HERBS: Add 2 to 3 tablespoons chopped fresh chives, dill, parsley, watercress, or prepared horseradish to the cheese mixture and blend well.

SMOKED SALMON: Add 2 tablespoons of shredded smoked salmon or lox and ½ teaspoon lemon juice to the cheese mixture and blend well. (Some people like to add a bit of minced raw onion.)

ANCHOVIES: Add 2 to 3 tablespoons anchovy paste and 1 teaspoon lemon juice to the cheese mixture and blend well. For canapés, garnish with capers.

MINCED CLAMS: Add a well-drained 8- to 10-ounce can of minced clams, 1 teaspoon lemon juice, and ½ teaspoon Worcestershire sauce to the cheese mixture. Blend well.

CHIPPED BEEF: Add ¼ cup of finely chipped dried beef, ½ teaspoon Dijon mustard, and a dash of Tabasco or hot pepper sauce to the cheese mixture. Blend well.

MINCED HAM: Add ¼ cup of finely minced or deviled ham, 1

tablespoon pickle relish, and 1 tablespoon mayonnaise to the cheese mixture. Blend well.

Other Cold Fillings

RED OR BLACK CAVIAR: Garnish with chopped hard-cooked egg, or a tiny dab of sour cream.

TUNA OR EGG SALAD: Especially good for larger tomatoes, pastry shells.

PREPARED CHEESE SPREADS: Some aren't all bad. Try Cheddar or Blue cheese spreads on celery.

DEVILED SARDINES: All you have to do is to drain a can of sardines (preferably skinless and boneless, but if not, just remove the long backbones) and using a fork, mix with ½ teaspoon Dijon mustard, ¼ teaspoon Worcestershire sauce, a few drops of lemon juice, a dash of Tabasco, and just enough mayonnaise to moisten.

STEAK TARTARE: As elegant a canapé as you can make (pages 134–135).

PISSALADIÈRE

A French version of the Neapolitan pizza, pissaladière is delightfully easy to make compared with the more involved classic version. It offers the cook without a kitchen a chance to make something out of the ordinary, and is hearty enough to keep hungry guests at bay while the rest of the dinner is being prepared. For a quick dough, I use the prepared refrigerated biscuits or rolls usually found in the dairy case of the supermarket.

> 1 recipe prepared pizza dough, or 1 8-ounce package refrigerated dough for crescent or other flaky rolls
> 3 medium onions, finely sliced
> 6 to 8 tablespoons olive oil
> 2 cloves garlic, finely minced
> ½ cup pizza or spaghetti sauce
> ½ cup coarsely chopped black olives
> 1 2-ounce can flat anchovy fillets

Preheat oven to 400 degrees. Lightly grease a flat glass or metal baking dish with olive oil. Remove the cylinder of dough from the can and unroll it in a single sheet; lightly press perforations together and do not separate the dough into individual segments. Place the sheet of dough in the baking pan, press it flat, and crimp the outer edges to form a raised lip. Set aside. Sauté the onions and garlic in about 4 tablespoons of the olive oil until golden brown. Spread a thin coating of pizza or spaghetti sauce evenly over the dough. Arrange the sautéed onions, chopped olives, and anchovy fillets over the sauce and sprinkle a few drops of the remaining olive oil on top. Bake for 15 minutes, or until browned. Cut into squares or wedges and serve hot.

Serves 6.

GRILLED LIVER PÂTÉ AND CHEESE HORS D'OEUVRES

These delicious grilled hors d'oeuvres are easy to prepare, especially in an electric broiler. Depending on appetites, allow 1 or 2 slices of toast per person.

- Sliced bread (any kind)
- Dijon mustard
- ½ pound braunschweiger or smoked liver sausage (the soft kind)
- ½ pound sliced Swiss or Cheddar cheese
- Mayonnaise

Trim the crusts from the bread and toast very lightly. Spread each slice first with mustard, and then with liver sausage. Top with a slice of cheese, with a dollop of mayonnaise in the center. Place under the broiler (not too close to the coil or flame) until the cheese begins to melt and the mayonnaise begins to brown. Cut each slice into quarters, if you wish, and serve at once.

Serves 8.

PASTRY SHELLS:
HOT HORS D'OEUVRES FOR THE EXHIBITIONIST

Showing off is part of the personality of every good cook. First place for really fancy hors d'oeuvres should go to filled pastry shells; they are at least a close second to Beluga caviar. French in origin, they require a deft hand and a lot of practice, not to mention the marble slab that many pastry chefs say is the only way to make the flaky dough. Starting from scratch is a bit beyond the cook without a kitchen.

Nevertheless, most areas will have a bakery that sells them or at least a supermarket where you can find frozen shells ready for baking. Fillings can be almost anything that will fit into the size you buy (these range from very tiny ones the size of a silver dollar to large ones which can be used for luncheons as an entrée). Just remember to drain your filling well, and make sure that the shells are baked to a light golden brown before filling so that they remain crisp. (If you use the frozen kind, follow package directions.) Figure about 3 to 5 per person as an appetizer, if they are small, 2 to 3 if they are larger.

Start with a cup of thick béchamel (page 81) or mornay sauce (page 82). You can use any of the following as a filling (all should be cooked beforehand): Chopped mushrooms, asparagus tips, tiny shrimp, minced crab, clams, ham, chicken, turkey, or dried beef. Spoon the filling into each shell, leaving room for the sauce to be poured on top without running over. Drop the sauce into each with a teaspoon, and arrange them without touching each other on a baking sheet, or on foil over a broiler pan. Put under a preheated broiler a minute or two—just long enough to make them hot and bubbly, but be careful not to burn them.

Serve immediately.

8
Soups

In this era of convenience foods, canned and packaged soups are a sensible part of any larder. Many of them can be doctored up a bit to make a distinctive first course with a minimum of effort.

Adding a tablespoon of curry powder to a can of condensed cream of chicken soup can make a decent version of the French Senegalese. Also try adding a tablespoon of curry powder to cream of asparagus or cream of celery condensed soup, made according to the instructions on the label. A pat of butter in the center of each bowl makes a richer soup.

If you've made a baked ham, save the bone. Add it to prepared split pea soup (either the canned condensed variety or the packaged dry ingredients), simmer a little longer than usual, and you'll have a much more flavorful soup.

Some kinds of canned soups are so good that it's not worth the time and trouble to make them yourself. Black bean soup is a good example, if you can find it. The once-available popular brands seem to have disappeared from the supermarkets, but you may be able to find them in gourmet food stores. With a dash of sherry stirred into its dark velvety smoothness and a thin slice of lemon floating on top, canned black bean soup makes an unusual and tasty beginning for a meal.

Still, nothing beats homemade soups, and you don't have to be a master chef to make them. They can add a hearty touch to a simple meal, and are generally inexpensive to prepare if budget is a concern.

BASIC STOCK

A clear soup that is part of hundreds of other recipes, stock (or bouillon) is easy to make. If you need cooked meat or chicken for a particular recipe (chicken salad, for example), you can make your own stock in the process. You should use about 3 cups of meat or chicken, along with a few shin or marrow bones or chicken backs and necks. Then all you need to do is add some vegetables and seasonings to give character to the stock. A few celery stalks and tops, carrots, onions, leeks, and turnips are good. Add a teaspoon of salt, a few whole peppercorns, a bay leaf, a few sprigs of parsley or dill (or both), and ½ teaspoon of rosemary or thyme. Put everything into a large pot, cover with 1½ to 2 quarts of water and bring to a boil. Then lower the heat, cover, and simmer slowly for 2 to 3 hours to get the maximum flavor. Remove the meat and the larger vegetables, salt to taste, and strain through a colander. For a very clear stock, strain again through a double layer of cheesecloth, then cool and refrigerate. Take off the solidified fat after it chills. If you make chicken stock, you may want to save the fat to use in matzo balls (page 105) or other recipes. Stock can be frozen for future use.

FRENCH ONION SOUP GRATINÉE

French onion soup is available in dried concentrated form as well as in cans, but it can be made at home without too much trouble and is well worth the effort. The melted cheese topping or gratinée (which can also be used on store-bought onion soup) adds a nice touch; it is easy to prepare but requires an oven or electric broiler.

- ½ pound large yellow or Spanish onions, very thinly sliced
- 3 tablespoons butter
- 1 quart beef bouillon or stock
- Salt and pepper to taste
- 4 slices French bread, toasted
- ¼ pound Gruyère or Swiss cheese, grated
- Grated Parmesan cheese

Cook the onions in the butter until they are golden brown, about 15 minutes over low heat. Add the bouillon and simmer slowly for another 20 to 30 minutes, until the onions are very tender. Add salt and pepper to taste. To make the gratinée, pour the soup into heatproof bowls, float a slice of toasted bread in each, and spinkle with a generous layer of grated Gruyère cheese. Brown in a hot oven for about 5 minutes, until the cheese is lightly browned and melted. (If you use an electric broiler, set it on medium heat and keep an eye on the soup to make sure it doesn't burn.) Serve, and pass the grated Parmesan at the table.

Serves 4.

GAZPACHO

Native to Spain, gazpacho has achieved a certain fame in America among people who genuinely care about food. And no wonder! Essentially a finely chopped salad in a delicious chilled broth, there are few things as satisfying on a hot summer day as this refreshing iced Andalusian soup. (It is really so delicate and inventive, I am surprised that the French haven't claimed it as their own!)

Like so many good dishes, there are at least two dozen versions, all claiming to be the genuine article. My version might not be authentic, but it is easy and so good that it is the only one I keep making.

A few pointers before starting: Instead of the water or tomato juice base sometimes used, which makes the soup taste either too insipid or too acid, I use chicken stock as a base. This can be canned or homemade, but in either case should be fat-free. I like College Inn canned chicken broth, which is very flavorful and has practically no fat. If you use another kind, make sure to chill it first and skim the congealed fat from the surface before using it. Also, try to use locally grown, vine-ripened tomatoes. This may limit the months when you'll be able to make gazpacho, but I've found that it has no real zing if made with hothouse tomatoes.

The time-honored method of preparing the raw vegetables (and the way I learned to do it) is to chop them in a wooden bowl, using an old-fashioned curved-blade chopping knife. But time marches on, and a blender will do the trick almost as well. Remember, however, that the vegetables are supposed to be slightly crunchy, so be careful not to reduce them to a smooth purée. Once you've taken the blender down from the top shelf, you might as well make a big batch—gazpacho is ideal for the first day of a camping trip or to whip up in a boat galley, since no cooking is needed, but it should be kept cold.

> 4 large, very ripe tomatoes, peeled and cut into pieces
> 1 medium onion, minced
> 2 large cucumbers, peeled and cut into slices
> 2 cloves garlic, minced
> Juice of 1 lemon (or more to taste)
> 3 tablespoons olive oil
> 1 teaspoon salt
> Freshly ground black pepper to taste
> 1 quart fat-free chicken broth
> Herb-flavored croutons; chopped scallions; thinly sliced onion rings or cucumber slices; or sour cream (use one or more for garnish)

Put all the ingredients, except the garnishes, into a blender and turn the controls on and off until everything is finely chopped but not puréed. (You will probably have to do it in several stages, using some of the chicken broth in each batch to keep the mixture buoyant.) Mix the batches together in a large serving bowl. If the gazpacho is too thick, add more broth or a few small ice cubes. Serve it ice cold, plain or garnished with croutons, chopped scallions, or additonal onions and cucumbers. A spoonful of sour cream on the top is a nice contrast of flavor and texture.

Serves 8 to 10, or 6 really hungry people.

STRACCIATELLA ALLA ROMANA

I must admit that one of the reasons I am including this recipe is because of the jaw-breaking name. It is really simple as pie and quick as a wink to prepare. It is remarkably similar to Chinese egg drop soup, but without the addition of cornstarch as a thickener. In Italian, the name literally means "Rags, Roman Style."

3 eggs
4 tablespoons freshly grated Parmesan cheese
6 cups chicken broth (canned, if you wish)
Chopped parsley or chives

Beat the eggs thoroughly with a fork, and then stir in the cheese and parsley (or chives). Bring the chicken broth to a rolling boil, and then dribble the egg mixture into the boiling soup, stirring constantly until the eggs congeal in little threads. Serve immediately.

Serves 4 to 6.

AVGOLEMONO

(Greek Egg and Lemon Soup)

Very easy to make, avgolemono is a deliciously different soup, with the tangy taste of lemon in counterpoint to the delicacy of the chicken broth.

½ cup raw rice
6 cups chicken broth or stock
3 eggs, beaten
Juice of 2 lemons
Salt and pepper to taste
Diced cooked chicken (optional)
¼ cup chopped parsley

Cook the rice in the broth for 15 to 20 minutes, or until it is tender. Drizzle 2 cups of the hot broth very, very slowly into the beaten eggs, stirring briskly to make sure the eggs do not curdle into separate wisps. Pour the egg-broth mixture into the pot of broth and rice. Stir in the lemon juice and season with salt and pepper to taste. Add diced pieces of cooked chicken, if desired. Heat, but do not boil, Serve garnished with the chopped parsley.

Serves 4 to 6.

JEWISH CHICKEN SOUP

Known amusingly as "Jewish penicillin," this classic soup is easy to make anywhere there is a source of heat and a large pot. Chicken soup is often served with one of several additions, a traditional favorite being the delicious dumplings known as matzo balls. (Directions follow the recipe.) Other classic additions include kreplach, small meat-filled pockets of dough that are very similar to ravioli or wontons. They are rather complicated to make in limited space, but meat ravioli, available frozen and without sauce, make an acceptable substitute.

Cooked rice or fine egg noodles can also vary the basic chicken soup. Cook them according to package directions. You may also want to try adding pastina, or any number of other tiny pastas, as well as barley and dried mushrooms, to the soup stock. Follow package instructions for cooking times.

- 3- to 4-pound stewing chicken, cut into pieces
- Liver and giblets from the chicken
- 3 carrots, cut into 2-inch pieces
- 4 stalks celery, including tops, cut into 2-inch pieces
- 4 small onions, peeled
- 2 leeks or 1 small bunch of scallions, cut into 2-inch pieces
- 2 cloves garlic, split (optional)
- 1 tablespoon salt
- 8 peppercorns
- ½ bunch fresh parsley
- ½ bunch fresh dill

Wash the chicken under cold running water. Put it into the pot and add cold water to cover (6 cups or more). Bring the water to a boil and add the liver and giblets, carrots, celery, onions, leeks, garlic, salt, and peppercorns. Cook until the chicken is tender (approximately 1½ hours, though the timing may vary from one fowl to another). Add the parsley and dill about 15 minutes before turning off the heat. Correct the seasonings. You can remove the skin and cut the chicken into smaller pieces if you wish. Skim off scum and excess fat if necessary.

Serves 6 to 8.

Matzo Balls

2 tablespoons rendered chicken fat (schmaltz)
½ cup matzo meal
2 eggs, beaten
1 teaspoon salt
¼ teaspoon white pepper, or to taste

To render chicken fat, heat excess fat trimmed from the chicken in a small pan, pouring it off into a heatproof container as it melts. Cool.

Mix together the matzo meal, eggs, chicken fat, salt, and pepper, blending well with a fork, Add 2 tablespoons for cold water and blend. Cover the bowl and refrigerate for at least 1 hour. When thoroughly chilled, form into balls the size of golf balls and ease gently into a large pot of a slowly-boiling salted water. (They will expand to double their size while cooking.) Cook covered for about 30 minutes. Remove them gently from the water with a slotted spoon and serve in the chicken soup.

Serves 4 to 6.

COLD SPINACH SOUP

This version of the classic Russian-Jewish schav can be made with spinach, escarole, sorrel, or broccoli. It can be prepared well in advance and will keep nicely in the refrigerator. it is perfect on a picnic, served in glasses from a thermos.

1 pound fresh spinach (escarole, broccoli, or sorrel)
1 teaspoon salt
6 cups water or clear chicken broth
2 eggs, beaten

Juice of 2 lemons
1 teaspoon sugar
Garnishes:
Sour cream
Hot tiny new potatoes
Chopped cucumbers
Fresh dill
Chopped scallions

Thoroughly wash the spinach (or other vegetables), discarding the stems. Chop coarsely. Combine salt and water (or broth) and bring to a boil. Add the chopped spinach and simmer for approximately 5 minutes. Beat the eggs in a large bowl. Slowly drizzle some of the hot liquid into the eggs, stirring briskly with a fork so the eggs do not congeal. Gradually add at least two cups of the hot liquid to the eggs, stirring constantly until it is a creamy color, without shreds of egg showing. Stir the egg mixture into the hot soup, and add the lemon juice and sugar. Allow to cool before refrigerating. (You can speed the cooling by immersing the pot in a sink filled with cold water, but take care not to allow it to tip.)

Serve chilled, topped with any of the garnishes suggested. With a dollop of sour cream and a sprinkling of fresh dill and chopped cumcumbers, it makes an ideal summer refresher.

Serves 4 to 6.

CAPE COD CLAM CHOWDER

2 onions, finely chopped
3 tablespoons butter or margarine
2 10-ounce cans minced clams, including broth (or 1 can minced clams and 1 can whole clams, including broth)
1½ cups diced cooked new potatoes
½ cup diced cooked carrots
½ cup diced cooked celery
2 cups milk
1 cup light cream or half-and-half
Salt and pepper to taste

Sauté the onions in the butter for 5 minutes, or until lightly browned. Add the clam broth and the cooked vegetables. (You can use already cooked fresh or frozen vegetables, left over from another meal, or cooked them in the clam broth for approximately 10 minutes.) Add the clams, milk, cream, and salt and pepper to taste, and simmer for another 5 minutes. Stir occasionally while simmering. Serve with oyster crackers.

Serves 4.

COLD HUNGARIAN CHERRY SOUP

This unusual dish is a refreshing summer starter with a sweet-and-sour taste.

>2 pounds canned sour cherries, pitted
>2 tablespoons cornstarch
>1 cup cold water
>¼ to ½ cup sugar, to taste
>1 cup sour cream
>½ cup dry red wine, or juice of 1 lemon

Put the cherries and their liquid into a small saucepan. Mix together the cornstarch and water, and add to the cherries. Bring to a boil over low heat and simmer for 3 to 5 minutes until the liquid thickens. Remove from the heat, stir in the sugar, and chill thoroughly, Add the sour cream and wine (or lemon juice) as you are about to serve, stirring it in thoroughly, and float an extra dollop of sour cream on the top.

Serves 4.

9
Salads

An entire repertoire of different salads are particularly worthwhile for cooking without a kitchen. From a simple mixed green salad with your meal to a combination of meats, cheese, and almost anything else in what is referred to as a chef's salad, all of them can be made with the most rudimentary equipment and will be popular with almost everyone.

The more elaborate salads, like Salade Niçoise, can be a main dish for a summer supper or luncheon. They are also a boon to the galley cook, who can do most of the preparation in advance or at home, bringing ingredients on board in a cooler. Fruit salads can be served as desserts with a scoop of sherbet in the center or as the beginning to a meal of chicken or fish. (A fruit or vegetable salad with cottage cheese is a favorite with dieters.)

SALADE NIÇOISE

Here is a salad that really is served as a entrée. It is perfect on a summer's day, especially by the sea, where one can be reminded of Nice, on the French Riviera, which gave its name to this easy and distinctive dish.

Boston or other leaf lettuce
2 cups cold cooked green beans (slightly undercooked, so they are still a bit crunchy)
1 cup diced cooked potatoes
1 6½-ounce can of tuna, drained

3 medium tomatoes, cut into wedges
1 mild onion, thinly sliced (optional)
1 2-ounce can rolled anchovies, drained
½ cup black olives (preferably the oil-packed Greek variety)
4 hard-cooked eggs
½ cup (approximately) classic French vinaigrette dressing (page 76)
Salt and pepper to taste

Line a large bowl with lettuce leaves and arrange the cooked green beans, diced potatoes, tuna, and tomatoes on the lettuce. Separate the onion slices into rings and distribute on top, dotting these with the rolled anchovies and black olives. Slice the hard-cooked eggs or cut into wedges like the tomatoes and arrange decoratively around the bowl. When ready to serve, bring the bowl to the table and pour approximately ½ cup of the dressing over the salad. Mix thoroughly but gingerly and season with salt and pepper.

Serves 4.

CAESAR SALAD

Caesar salad is one of the great classic salads, and at least a dozen restaurants from New York to Tijuana swear they originated the recipe. The following is a composite of the best "original" recipes, with a minimum of folderol.

3 medium heads romaine lettuce
1 cup croutons or bread cut into small cubes
¾ cup olive oil
4 to 6 tablespoons grated Parmesan cheese
1 clove garlic (optional)
3 tablespoons wine vinegar
Juice of 1 lemon
1 egg, cooked for 1 minute in its shell
½ teaspoon salt
½ teaspoon coarsely ground black pepper
1 2-ounce can rolled anchovies, drained (optional)

Wash and thoroughly dry the romaine. Keep well chilled. Toss croutons with 2 tablespoons olive oil in a frying pan over low heat until they are golden brown, then roll them in some of the Parmesan cheese until lightly coated. Set aside to cool. Break the crisp romaine into a deep salad bowl that you have rubbed with a bruised garlic clove. Pour the remaining olive oil, vinegar, and lemon juice over the romaine. Add the egg and sprinkle on the salt, pepper, and remaining Parmesan cheese. Toss lightly. Arrange the toasted croutons around the edge of the bowl and garnish with the rolled anchovies, tossing again at the very last minute. Serve on chilled plates, if possible.

Serves 4 to 6.

SPINACH AND MUSHROOM SALAD

This is a very interesting salad, either as a luncheon entrée or with a simple roasted chicken or roast beef for dinner.

1 clove garlic (optional)
½ teaspoon dry or prepared (Dijon-style) mustard
½ teaspoon salt
½ teaspoon freshly ground black pepper
4 tablespoons lemon juice
½ cup olive or salad oil
½ pound fresh mushrooms
1 pound fresh spinach
1 bunch scallions (green onions)
¼ pound bacon
1 hard-cooked egg (optional)

Use a wooden or ceramic bowl large enough to toss the salad well. Crush the clove of garlic and rub it around the inside of the bowl. Mix the mustard, salt, pepper, and lemon juice in the bottom of the bowl. Add the oil and mix again. (A few drops of water will help to homogenize this mixture.) Cut the mushrooms into ½-inch thick slices, trimming the stems first. Toss these in the salad dressing mixture to marinate while you prepare the rest of the ingredients.

Wash and dry the spinach thoroughly. (Spinach is always sandy, so be sure to wash it thoroughly in running water, if you can.) Discard the stems and any wilted leaves. Cut the scallions into ½-inch pieces, including the green tops.

Fry the bacon slowly, starting with a cold frying pan. After it is thoroughly done, drain on paper towels or brown paper, cool and then crumble. Toss ingredients together well and serve, garnishing the top with finely grated cooked egg if you wish.

Serves 4 to 6.

WILTED SPINACH SALAD

A variation of the spinach and mushroom salad can be made by tossing the ingredients in the frying pan used to cook the bacon. First pour off most of the drippings and toss just long enough to make the spinach wilt slightly. Some people like to add a teaspoon of sugar while tossing to give the salad a slightly sweet–sour flavor.

TARAMA SALAD
(Salted Fish Roe Spread or Dip)

This Greek and Turkish specialty is generally available only in gourmet shops and in Greek neighborhoods, but if you can find it, get it. Some stores will carry a prepared tarama ready for serving, which is called taramasalata. One brand available in some parts of the country is Fantis. The roe itself is the color of smoked salmon; the prepared variety is a light pink color. The salted fish roe when prepared should be the consistency of thick mayonnaise. It is delicious served in a Middle Eastern antipasto, as the center of a plate with sliced cucumbers, tomato wedges, Greek black olives, pickled peppers and Feta cheese (also available in gourmet shops). It is very salty, so have plenty of chilled white wine or beer ready. If you prefer a less salty spread, mix the tarama with 2 cups of water, then strain it carefully in a very fine sieve, being sure to drain all the water before using. You can make it by hand, but the following blender method is much quicker and easier.

- 1 10-ounce jar of tarama
- Juice of 1 lemon (or more, to taste)
- 1 clove garlic, minced (optional)
- ½ cup crumbled fresh bread
- 1 cup olive oil
- ¼ cup chopped parsley

Making the tarama spread is very much like making mayonnaise. Begin by putting approximately half of the tarama and lemon juice in the blender with the garlic and the bread crumbs. Start the blender (slowest speed) and add the oil in a slow, steady stream. The mixture will thicken like mayonnaise. After it begins to homogenize, add the rest of the tarama and more lemon juice, to taste. The mixture should be pale pink and fluffy. Arrange in a mound on an attractive serving dish and garnish with chopped parsley and lemon wedges if desired. It must be refrigerated until ready to use. It may be served with crackers, French bread, or if possible, with flat, round Near Eastern bread (called pita).

Serves 6.

GUACAMOLE
(Mexican Avocado Salad and Dip)

2 large, very ripe avocados
1 tablespoon grated onion
1 medium-size ripe tomato, diced
Juice of ½ lemon
1 clove garlic, finely chopped
1 teaspoon Tabasco sauce
Salt and pepper to taste

Peel and mash the avocados. Add the onion and tomato. Mix in the remaining ingredients. Blend thoroughly, but don't be concerned with making it smooth—it should have a chunky consistency. Keep chilled until ready to serve. Serve in hollowed-out tomatoes as a salad, or with tortilla chips as a dip. Weight watchers take note: Avocados are very high in calories.

Serves 4 as a salad, or 6 as an appetizer.

COLE SLAW

A substantial alternative to a salad, cole slaw can be made in advance and kept in the refrigerator until needed. It is ideal for boating and picnics because of its compactness.

4 cups shredded cabbage (red cabbage makes an attractive change)
1 or 2 carrots, shredded
½ cup mayonnaise
Juice of ½ lemon
1 teaspoon celery seeds or caraway seeds (whichever you prefer)
Salt and pepper to taste

Combine all ingredients well and toss to distribute mayonnaise. Cover and refrigerate until you are ready to use it. Cole slaw will keep for at least 2 days.

Serves 6 to 8.

CUCUMBER AND YOGURT SALAD

3 large cucumbers
2 cups plain yogurt
¼ cup olive oil
2 teaspoons lemon juice
Salt and pepper to taste
Chopped fresh mint leaves or fresh dill

Wash and peel the cucumbers and slice them into uniformly thin rounds. Mix the yogurt, olive oil, lemon juice, salt, and pepper in a bowl and add the cucumber slices. Toss lightly and serve garnished with mint or dill. (If necessary, dried dill or mint leaves can be used, crumbling them between the palms of your hands onto the salad.)

Serves 4.

Variations

Use a cup of sour cream instead of yogurt. (My mother uses this sour cream dressing on a mixed garden salad and wryly refers to it as "farmer's chop suey.")

Use tomato chunks and radishes as well as cucumbers.

CURRIED TUNA AND EGG SALAD

This tuna salad with a difference can be brought to a picnic or made anywhere you go. As with anything made with mayonnaise, however, but sure to keep it cool until ready to serve. I suggest using salad olives for a practical reason: economy. Since the olives will be cut up in the salad anyway, there is no reason to buy the more expensive kind that are prettily arranged in the bottle—salad olives are the same thing, but with some broken bits mixed in, and at a much lower cost.

1 6½-ounce can tuna, drained and flaked
1 medium green pepper, diced
½ cup salad olives or small stuffed green olives,
    coarsely chopped
3 to 4 tablespoons mayonnaise
1 teaspoon curry powder
3 hard-cooked eggs, chopped
Thinly sliced lemon, chopped parsley, cherry tomatoes
    (for garnish)

Combine the flaked tuna, diced green pepper and chopped olives in a bowl. Mix the mayonnaise and curry powder together and blend thoroughly, then add to the tuna mixture and stir well. Add the chopped eggs and mix lightly, just until evenly distributed. Decorate with any of the garnishes suggested and keep refrigerated, or at least cool, until you are ready to serve.
    Serves 3 to 4.

10
The Egg and You

There are pros and cons about eggs: Some people believe they have too much cholesterol for our diet, while others insist they are a very good source of protein. You'll have to decide for yourself, but in the meantime, here are a variety of easy-to-prepare dishes that can be served as brunch, luncheon, and supper entrées. Eggs are perfectly suited to the limitations of the small (or nonexistent) kitchen—they cook quickly and can be used in a huge variety of ways, often changing their character completely with the substitution of just a few ingredients. The recent vogue for egg-rich crepes of all kinds is merely the latest facet of the perennial popularity of eggs.

Whatever the dish, strictly fresh eggs are essential. Another bit of advice: Always try to beat and season eggs just before you are ready to cook them. (The recipes that follow use large or extra-large eggs.)

Eggs Cooked Plain and Simple

You'd be amazed how many people don't know how to boil, poach, or fry an egg—and are embarrassed to ask. These three basic methods of cooking eggs are a cinch. Here's how.

SOFT- AND HARD-COOKED EGGS

Place the eggs in a pot of cold, salted water, and bring to a boil. Turn the heat down and boil very gently for 3 to 4 minutes for soft-cooked eggs, or from 12 to 15 minutes for hard-cooked.

Plunge the eggs immediately into cold water to stop the cooking process and to make them easier to shell.

POACHED EGGS

Break eggs carefully to keep yolks intact and ease them, one at a time, into simmering, lightly salted water, which has been stirred into a "whirlpool" to keep the whites together. Cook for 3 to 5 minutes, depending on how you prefer them. Remove from the water carefully, using a slotted spoon. If necessary, eggs can be poached a little ahead of time; to reheat, slip them into simmering salted water for half a minute or less just before serving.

FRIED EGGS

Melt enough butter to generously coat the bottom of a heavy frying pan. When the butter begins to foam, turn the heat to medium-low and carefully break the eggs into the pan. Cook until the whites become solidified. If you like your eggs fried on both sides (known as "over easy"), turn carefully with a spatula and cook a half minute or more, then remove carefully and serve.

Variations on a Theme

DEVILED EGGS

These make a tasty luncheon or supper dish, served on a bed of greens, with crisp green pepper rings, wedges of tomatoes and rolled slices of cold Virginia ham or rare roast beef. Use 2 eggs per serving. They are also excellent as an appetizer.

    8 hard-cooked eggs
    ⅓ cup mayonnaise
    1 teaspoon Dijon mustard

1 teaspoon lemon juice
1 teaspoon Worcestershire sauce
Dash of Tabasco (red pepper) sauce
2 teaspoons well-drained pickle relish, chopped capers, or chopped black olives
Salt and pepper to taste
Chopped parsley, paprika, pimientos, or anchovies (for garnish)

Slice the hard-cooked eggs in half lengthwise and carefully remove the yolks. Mash the egg yolks with the remaining ingredients, except the garnishes. Fill the egg whites with the mixture, and garnish with chopped parsley, paprika, pimientos, or anchovies (or any combination of these). Chill before serving.

Serves 4.

Variations

Add a teaspoon of your favorite curry powder to the egg yolk mixture.

Add 1 tablespoon chili powder to the egg yolk mixture.

DEVILED EGGS IN ASPIC

This is a real show-stopper, and very easy to make for a buffet or a supper party. Be sure to buy jellied consommé or tomato-flavored madrilène. Use a 1½ quart ring mold.

8 deviled eggs (pages 118–119)
2 cans jellied consommé or madrilène
2 tablespoons sherry or cognac
Pimiento strips, slivered cooked ham, chicken, or anchovy fillets (optional)
Parsley or watercress (for garnish)

Heat 1 can of consommé or madrilène, add 1 tablespoon of the sherry (or cognac), pour into the mold and chill until it jells again. In the meantime, make the deviled eggs, but instead of mounding the filling, fill each cavity until level and put the halves back together, securing with a toothpick. Heat the remaining can of consommé only until it liquifies, add the remaining tablespoon of sherry or cognac and set aside to cool—but do not let it set. Place the eggs (and your choice of pimiento strips, slivered cooked ham, or chicken, etc.) evenly around the mold on top of the solidified consommé. Then carefully pour the cooled consommé over the eggs to cover. Chill until firm—at least 2 hours. To unmold, dip very quickly in warm water, then reverse on a serving platter. Garnish with sprigs of parsley or watercress, and serve on lettuce leaves, with tomatoes, carrot strips, and celery.

Serves 4 to 6.

EGGS BENEDICT

4 slices Canadian bacon
1 tablespoon butter or margarine
2 English muffins, halved and toasted
4 eggs, poached (page 118)
1 cup prepared or mock hollandaise sauce (page 81)
Pitted black olives

Fry the Canadian bacon slowly in the butter. When cooked, place a slice on each toasted English muffin half. Put a poached egg on top of the Canadian bacon, cover with hollandaise sauce and garnish with black olives. Serve hot. (You may wish to put these under the broiler for a minute or so to brown the tops.)

Serves 4.

EGGS FLORENTINE

2 10-ounce packages frozen chopped spinach, cooked
   for 5 minutes and well drained
4 tablespoons butter
4 eggs, poached (page 118)
1 cup mornay sauce (page 82)
Nutmeg (freshly ground, if possible)

Melt the butter on the hot cooked spinach. For each serving, place a mound of spinach in a shallow baking dish or individual ramekin. Place a poached egg on top, and cover with the mornay sauce. Sprinkle lightly with nutmeg, and put under the broiler for a few minutes to brown the tops.
   Serves 4.

Omelets

Beginning with a basic omelet, there are virtually limitless combinations that can be made for plain and fancy lunches or suppers in a hurry: spinach, mushroom, almost any kind of cheese, cooked meat and seafood, jelly or preserves for a dessert omelet. Omelets are easy to make over a campfire or in a boat's galley as well as at home.

For a soft omelet, add 1 teaspoon of cold water for each egg or add a few bits of soft butter to the beaten eggs before cooking. Use very fresh eggs at room temperature, mixing with a fork until the whites and yolks are just combined. Since an omelet continues to cook from accumulated internal heat, be sure not to cook it too long. Remove it from the pan to warm plates when the surface is still shiny. It will be done by the time it is on the table.

When making an omelet, figure on 2 large eggs per person. Depending on the size of your pan, it is better to make 2 smaller omelets than one large one, but don't ever attempt to use more than 8 eggs at a time. Use a heavy pan with sloping sides and a rounded bottom. Start with just enough butter to coat the bottom of the pan, since too much butter will make the omelet taste greasy.

Generally, fillings for omelets should be cooked first, then added to the eggs at room temperature. To keep the omelet light, add no more than ¼ cup of filling per person. Be sure to wipe the pan clean after sautéing ingredients. If they stick to the bottom, the pan should be washed before frying the eggs to make the omelet more manageable. If the filling is juicy, be sure to drain or cook off any excess liquid before mixing with the eggs, to keep the omelet from being too runny.

BASIC OMELET

8 eggs (at room temperature)
½ teaspoon salt
¼ teaspoon freshly ground pepper
Butter

Beat the eggs, salt, and pepper with a fork or wire whisk until the whites and yolks are just blended—about a half minute should do it. Heat about 1 tablespoon of butter over a low heat in the pan, just enough to coat the bottom of the pan. Raise the heat to moderately high and when the butter starts to bubble, add the eggs. (If at all possible, make the omelet in 2 batches.) As the omelet begins to set, pull the edges toward the center, letting the liquid flow onto the pan, until the omelet is just solid, but still shiny on top. Dot the top with a few bits of butter and gently fold it in half with a spatula. Serve immediately on warm plates.

Serves 4.

SPINACH AND CHEESE OMELET

Mix the ingredients for a basic omelet, and add ½ cup well drained cooked spinach (either chopped or creamed), ¼ cup grated Cheddar or Swiss cheese, and ¼ teaspoon freshly grated nutmeg. Stir well. Cook as for the basic omelet.

Serves 4.

TOMATO OMELET

Melt 2 to 3 tablespoons butter in a frying pan. Chop 2 medium-size tomatoes and add to the pan with 1 teaspoon dry basil or dill (or 2 to 3 teaspoons fresh basil or dill). Cook over moderate heat, stirring well, until the tomatoes are pulpy and the juices have cooked off. Cool slightly and add to the ingredients for a basic omelet, mixing just until blended. Wash and dry the pan, then add more butter, and cook as for the basic omelet.
Serves 4.

MUSHROOM OMELET

Melt 2 tablespoons butter in a frying pan, add ½ cup sliced fresh mushrooms, and sauté quickly over medium high heat until tender. (You may also wish to add ¼ cup chopped scallions when browning the mushrooms.) Remove from the pan, and mix the ingredients for the basic omelet, stirring in the mushrooms, and cook as for the basic omelet; or, if desired, cook the basic omelet and add canned mushrooms as a topping just before serving.
Serves 4.

CURRIED ASPARAGUS AND CHEESE OMELET

Mix the ingredients for a basic omelet, adding 1 teaspoon of curry powder with the salt and pepper. Add ¼ cup drained cooked asparagus cut into 1-inch pieces, then stir in ¼ cup grated Swiss or Gruyère cheese and cook as for the basic omelet.

BACON OMELET

Beginning with a cold pan, fry 8 slices of bacon. When crisp, drain on paper towels, crumble, and mix into 1 recipe of the basic omelet. Wash and dry the pan, add butter, and cook as for basic omelet.
Serves 4.

HERB OMELETS

Mix the ingredients for 1 basic omelet. Add 1 to 1½ tablespoons dried herbs: fines herbes (parsley, chervil, and tarragon), herbes de Provence (an aromatic mixture from France, see page 69), dill, or summer savory. You may also use 2 to 3 tablespoons of fresh chopped herbs: chives, dill, or basil. Beat into the basic omelet and cook according to the basic recipe directions.

CAVIAR OMELET

This is a very special showy luncheon dish. You can use 4 ounces or less of red caviar (salmon roe), true sturgeon caviar (for the very rich), or lumpfish roe (which passes for caviar, but just barely). Make the basic omelet recipe, but instead of folding it, slide it onto a heated platter and fill the center with the caviar. Fold in the edges and serve with side dishes of chopped raw onion, lemon wedges, and sour cream.

Additional Fillings for Basic Omelets

The following suggestions can further vary the basic recipe. All additions should be either minced or chopped. They may be used as part of the omelet (see recipe for mushroom omelet) or spooned onto the flat omelet and folded (see recipe for caviar omelet), but be sure to heat the fillings thoroughly in melted butter in both cases. The proportion of ¼ cup per person should be maintained.

Seafood: Tiny shrimp, flaked tuna or other fish, crabmeat.

Cooked vegetables: Chopped artichoke hearts (not marinated), sautéed onions, scallions, broccoli tips, green peas.

Cooked meats: Almost any leftover meats—chicken, pork, ham, lamb, beef. (You may also wish to combine these with vegetables and/or cheese.)

Cheeses: Cheddar, Swiss, Blue or Roquefort, Parmesan. (Be sure that cheeses are grated into the raw eggs and mixed.)

DESSERT OMELETS

When using jellies and preserves, warm them first and spoon over the flat omelet, then fold (as for the caviar omelet). Use your favorite jelly or jam, possibly even hot fudge and marshmallows. These are especially liked by children. You may also wish to try well-drained canned or frozen fruits or minced fresh berries topped with slivered almonds or chopped walnuts, pecans, or peanuts.

Crepes

With the increasing popularity of crepes and filled pancakes, you can find ready-mixed crepe batters and dry mixes that just need milk added. The Russian-Jewish blintz is really just another crepe, filled with cheese.

BASIC CREPES

¾ cup sifted flour
Pinch of salt
3 eggs
5 tablespoons butter or margarine
¾ cup milk

Sift the flour into a mixing bowl, add the salt and eggs, one by one, beating with an egg beater or wire whisk until smooth. Add 3 tablespoons of melted butter and mix. Gradually add the milk until the mixture is the consistency of heavy cream. Let stand an hour or so in a cool place, then beat once more.

Lightly butter a small frying pan and pour in just enough batter to cover the bottom, tilting the pan to distribute the batter evenly. Fry with a moderate heat until the edges turn brown, then loosen with a spatula and carefully turn over and cook until just barely brown on the other side. Keep crepes warm on heated platter covered with a dish towel until ready to use. Makes 10 to 12 crepes.

Serves 4 to 6, depending on fillings.

Note: Don't be concerned if your first crepe does not turn out. If it is too runny, add more flour; if it is too thick, add more milk. The thinner you can make the crepes the better they will taste.

If you have pancake mix, you can also use it, thinned with extra milk.

Suggested Fillings for Crepes
Tuna or chicken salad
Ham and asparagus, covered with mornay sauce (page 82)
Chopped chicken livers (page 91)
Fruit compote (page 206)
Apricot preserves, chopped nuts, and sour cream

For other fillings, see the preceding pages with suggested omelet fillings.

Quiches

For a long time, this custardy dish was considered very fancy and difficult to make. Lately, though, more and more people have begun to discover how simple they actually are, and how satisfying—either as a supper dish or as an appetizer for a cocktail or dinner party. You'll need an oven for baking, but if you are cooking in cramped conditions and with limited utensils, don't bother making a pie crust. Buy a frozen pie crust or use a mix. I know this will strike dread in the hearts of the truly fastidious, but you'll be better off settling for the convenience of a prepared crust (and some brands are quite good).

QUICHE LORRAINE

1 9-inch pie shell (frozen or made from a mix)
4 eggs
1½ cups heavy cream
Salt and pepper to taste
Dash Tabasco sauce (optional)
¾ pound bacon, crisply fried and crumbled
2 tablespoons chopped chives (optional)
½ cup grated Swiss or Parmesan cheese
¼ teaspoon nutmeg

Prebake the pie shell according to the directions on the package. Then reduce the oven temperature to 350 degrees. Beat the eggs and add the cream, salt and pepper, and Tabasco sauce. Sprinkle the bacon, chives, and grated cheese over the bottom of the pie shell. Carefully pour the egg mixture over these ingredients and sprinkle the nutmeg on the top. Bake 20 to 30 minutes, or until a knife blade inserted into the center comes out clean. Allow to "set" for a few minutes to make cutting easier.

Serves 8 as an appetizer, or 4 as an entrée.

CRABMEAT QUICHE

Follow the directions for quiche Lorraine, substituting a 6½-ounce can of crabmeat (well drained) for the bacon, and omitting the chives.

ONION QUICHE

Follow the directions for quiche Lorraine, but instead of the bacon, use 1 large onion, coarsely chopped and sautéed in butter until lightly browned. Sprinkle chopped parsley over the quiche before serving.

MATZO BREI

This easy to make traditional Jewish dish can be served for brunch, but it makes an excellent luncheon dish or a substitute for rice or noodles with supper. Matzo is the unleavened bread eaten during Passover, but it is available in many supermarkets all year round. Poppy seeds are my own untraditional touch for a nice textural contrast.

- 8 matzos
- 4 eggs
- Salt and pepper
- 1 tablespoon poppy seeds
- 2 tablespoons butter (approximately)
- Sour cream

Break the matzos into small pieces in a bowl and cover with warm water for 30 seconds or so. Then pour off the water, making sure the matzo is well drained. Combine the eggs, a pinch of salt, a sprinkling of pepper, and the poppy seeds with the matzo, and mix with a fork. Heat about 1 tablespoon of the butter in a frying pan, and pour in the matzo and egg mixture. Fry over moderate heat for 2 to 3 minutes, until the bottom begins to brown. Carefully turn over, like a pancake. (If this proves difficult, you can break up the matzo brei and "scramble" it, like eggs.) Slide another tablespoon of butter underneath the matzo to coat the pan. Cook another 2 to 3 minutes and serve with dollops of sour cream. If you like sweet things, omit the salt and pepper and serve with jam or preserves.

Serves 4.

11
Entrées:
Barbecuing

Whether it is in your backyard, at the beach, or in the woods, there is nothing like a hearty meal barbecued outdoors. Here are a few guidelines to help make your al fresco meals trouble free.

First of all, it always seems that the coals are just right when all the cooking is finished. Avoid this problem by starting the charcoal at least 30 minutes before you are actually ready to begin cooking. Whatever kind of grill you use, the basic principle is the same: Start the fire with an electric or fluid lighter, and make sure that the coals are burned to a grayish-white ash before cooking, or your foods will taste unpleasantly of starter fluid.

When using a starter fluid, I have always found it helps to put a layer of newspaper under the coals. Light the paper after pouring the starter on the briquettes. If your grill has a vent on the underside, you can open and close it to control the air flow around the coals. Foods should be at least 3 inches above the coals. If they begin to burn, move the grill away from the heat, if possible.

Timetable for Typical Grilled Foods

BEEF

Steaks and unmarinated meats: Cut 1 to 1½ inches thick. Grill 5 minutes for rare to 15 minutes for well done. Turn once.

Shish kebobs and other skewered meats: Cut into 1-inch cubes. Marinate first, if desired, in one of the sauces on pages 84–87. Grill for 20 to 25 minutes. Turn once.

Hamburgers: Form into 1½-inch thick patties. Grill 5 minutes for rare to 10 minutes for well done. Turn once.

Tenderized meats (round steak, flank steak, chuck): Grill for 20 to 25 minutes, depending on thickness and degree of doneness desired. Turn once.

PORK

Rib or shoulder chops: Cut 1-inch thick. Grill at least 40 minutes, turning once.

Spareribs: Grill for 30 to 40 minutes, basting frequently with a sauce. Turn once.

Loin: Marinate or baste with sauce. Grill, turning often or on a revolving spit, for 40 to 50 minutes.

Cooked ham steaks: Grill for 15 minutes, turning once.

LAMB

Rib or shoulder chops: Cut 1½-inches thick. Grill for 25 minutes, turning once.

Kebobs: Marinate first, if desired. Grill for 20 minutes, turning once.

CHICKEN

Split or quartered: Grill for 45 minutes, basting frequently with a sauce. Turn once.

FISH

Whole small fish: Grill for 8 to 15 minutes, basting frequently with a sauce. Turn once.

Fish steaks: Cut 1 to 1½ inches thick. Grill for 12 to 15 minutes, basting frequently with a sauce.

VEGETABLES

Onions, zucchini: Rub with oil or butter, and wrap in aluminum foil. Place on grill for 30 to 40 minutes, or until soft when squeezed.

Tomatoes, mushrooms: Rub with oil or butter, and wrap in aluminum foil. Grill for 10 or 15 minutes.

Acorn squash: Cut in half, remove the seeds and put 1 tablespoon butter and 1 teaspoon brown sugar into each cavity. Wrap tightly in aluminum foil and place flat side up on grill for about 45 minutes, or until soft when squeezed.

Baked white and sweet potatoes: Wash the skins well, but do not peel. Rub them with butter or oil and wrap in aluminum foil. Place on the grill and roast for 45 minutes to 1 hour, turning from time to time. Test for doneness with a fork or skewer.

Corn: Remove the silk but not the husk. Soak the ears in cold water for half an hour, shake dry, wrap in aluminum foil and roast on the grill for about 15 to 20 minutes, turning often.

12

Entrées:

Beef

Whenever you are at a loss for what to serve, or the meal is for a diverse group, you cannot go wrong with a good roast beef. Served with oven-browned or French fried potatoes and a mixed green salad, it is a meal guaranteed to please just about anyone, no matter what their food prejudices.

When choosing a roast, try not to get one of less than 3 or 4 pounds. It will shrivel and become tough. (This is really not a major concern, since there are so many uses for cold roast beef—in sandwiches, curries, and salads—following its first appearance on your table.)

Choose a sirloin, tenderloin, rib, or rump roast with a good layer of fat on top. The beef should be at room temperature before roasting, if possible.

If you have a meat thermometer, it will indicate rare at 140 degrees, medium-rare at 150 degrees, medium at 160 degrees, and 170 degrees for well done.

CLASSIC ROAST BEEF

Allow at least half a pound raw weight per person; at least three-quarters of a pound per person for rib roasts.

>Sirloin, tenderloin, rib, or rump roast
Bacon or salt pork (if the roast is lean)
Salt and pepper
½ cup beef stock or bouillon
½ cup dry red wine

Preheat oven to 425 degrees. If there is not a layer of fat around the roast, tie strips of bacon or salt pork around it with white cotton cord. Place on a wire rack in a shallow baking pan. If you have a meat thermometer, stick it into the center of the roast. Place the roast in the oven for 30 minutes, then lower the heat to 350 degrees and continue to roast, basting frequently with the drippings from the bottom of the pan. Total time for rare should be between 12 and 15 minutes per pound; medium-rare to medium, between 15 and 17 minutes per pound; more than 18 minutes per pound for well done, although this toughens the meat. The roast should stand on a heated platter covered loosely with aluminum foil for about 10 minutes for ease in carving.

If you are serving Yorkshire pudding (see following recipe), make it at this time.

To make pan gravy, remove most of the fat in the pan, and add the bouillon-wine mixture to the pan. Place on stove or heat source, raise the heat to medium high and boil the liquid, stirring often with a wooden spoon to remove the browned particles from the bottom. After mixing, reduce the heat and allow to simmer for 5 to 7 minutes. Correct the seasoning with salt and pepper to taste.

Yorkshire Pudding

Anyone who says that the British are unimaginative cooks, has never had beautiful English roast beef and its traditional accompanying dish, Yorkshire pudding. Really just a variation of the popover, the pudding can be made at the same time as the beef, but should never be done ahead of time, because it gets soggy and dull. (There is also no reason why Yorkshire pudding cannot be served with other roasted meats, such as lamb, which have enough of the required drippings.)

¾ cup cold milk
½ cup flour
½ teaspoon salt
2 eggs, beaten
¼ cup roast beef or other meat drippings, or oil

Mix the cold milk, a little at a time, with the flour and salt, beating with an egg beater until smooth and creamy. Then add the beaten eggs and beat for 5 to 7 minutes until frothy. (Here's where an electric beater—or a good strong arm—comes in handy.) Refrigerate, or put in the coolest place you can, until thoroughly chilled. While this is being done, remove your roast from the oven and raise the heat to very hot (450 degrees). Pour about 1 teaspoon of drippings into each cup of a muffin tin and fill about half full with batter. (If you don't have a muffin tin, use a 9- by 13-inch baking pan.) Bake for 20 to 25 minutes. The puddings will puff up dramatically, but don't open the oven to check on them until they have baked for at least 20 minutes, or they will fall.

STEAK TARTARE

An elegant, haute cuisine dish (once you get used to the idea of eating raw meat), steak tartare is the subject of a now legendary story. A sweet young thing, taken to a fine restaurant by her gourmet-beau, wanted to seem worldly and sophisticated. When her escort ordered steak tartare, she said, "I'll have the same—and make mine medium!"

There are countless variations of this marvelous raw steak dish. The most important thing is to use the very best lean sirloin or top round steak, ground to order if possible, and without a bit of fat. If you can, buy it at the last possible moment to insure its freshness. Steak tartare is an excellent solution to the problem of creating a grand meal without a stove or refrigeration. For the most dramatic presentation, mix it at the table in a large wooden bowl. An extremely filling dish, you can usually figure that 1 pound of ground steak will serve 3 to 4 people (with a salad as the only side dish). Since it does not require cooking, you can also make it for an office party and serve it on small rounds of Melba toast or dark pumpernickel.

    2 pounds sirloin or top round steak, very lean and
       ground to order
    1 medium onion, finely chopped
    6 anchovies, mashed with a fork

2 tablespoons capers
2 tablespoons chopped fresh parsley
2 teaspoons Dijon mustard
Dash of Tabasco sauce
1 teaspoon Worcestershire sauce
1 tablespoon olive oil
5 tablespoons Cognac or vodka (optional)
Salt and pepper to taste
2 raw egg yolks
Chopped hard-cooked eggs for garnish (optional)

If you wish to prepare it first, put the meat in a large bowl and break it up with a fork. Add all the ingredients, except for the salt, pepper, and raw egg yolks, and stir lightly with a fork. Season with salt and pepper to taste. Then add the egg yolks and mix thoroughly. Mound into a smooth oval in the center of a platter, garnish with chopped hard-cooked eggs, if desired, and trim with sprigs of parsley.

If you want to make this at the table, arrange the various ingredients attractively on a tray; or combine all the ingredients, except for the raw egg yolks, beforehand, and nestle the eggs in a depression in the center. Then complete the preparations as described.

Serve with dry red wine, beer, or iced vodka.

Serves 6 to 8.

STEAK AU POIVRE
(French Pepper Steak)

To confound you, there are actually two completely different kinds of recipes called pepper steak. This version, the French steak au poivre, is a pungent dish made by covering a good steak with cracked black peppercorns and pan-frying it in hot butter and brandy. The other kind of pepper steak (page 137) is the familiar stir-fried Chinese dish made with another kind of pepper—the succulent sweet green or red vegetable.

This recipe will serve 2 people, but can be multiplied if your pan is big enough for an additional steak.

1 1- to 1¼-pound boneless steak (rib, club or sirloin)
Black peppercorns
1½ tablespoons olive oil
1½ tablespoons butter
½ teaspoon cornstarch
⅓ cup dry red wine
2 to 3 tablespoons brandy or cognac
Garlic juice or 1 clove garlic (optional)
Salt to taste

Trim the fat from the steak. Crush the peppercorns coarsely. Since ordinary preground or freshly milled pepper is too fine, experiment with your pepper mill to see if you can adjust the grind to the consistency of coffee grounds or heavier. If that doesn't work, use a mortar and pestle (if you have one), or put the peppercorns in a dish towel and crush them by rolling firmly with a rolling pin. Cover both sides of the steak with a coating of the crushed pepper, pressing it firmly into the meat. Heat the oil and butter in a large frying pan over high heat. Add the steak. The high temperature will sear the meat and keep the juices inside. Turn over after a few minutes (a 1½-inch-thick steak should be rare in about 3 minutes per side). Remove the steak from the pan and keep warm on a heated platter. Mix the cornstarch with the wine and pour into the pan. Add the cognac or brandy and stir over a moderate temperature until the sauce begins to boil. You may also want to add a hint of garlic juice or a bruised clove of garlic (which should be removed before serving). Season with salt to taste and pour the sauce over the steak. Serve with a robust red wine, accompanied, perhaps, with crisp shoestring potatoes and a mixed green salad with a classic French vinaigrette dressing (page 76).

CHINESE PEPPER STEAK

Although it may not have a perfect Chinese pedigree, this is a popular and easy to fix dish, with an interesting counterpoint of crunchy green peppers and lean steak in a fragrant sauce.

> ½ to ¾ pound of very lean steak, cut into ½-inch cubes or strips
> ¼ cup soy sauce
> 1 tablespoon dry sherry or white wine
> ½ teaspoon honey
> ½ teaspoon ground ginger or 1 teaspoon minced fresh ginger
> 1 clove garlic, minced
> 3 tablespoons salad oil (preferably sesame oil or peanut oil)
> 2 medium *sweet* green peppers, cut into strips about 2 inches long and ½ inch wide
> 4 scallions, cut into ½-inch pieces
> ½ teaspoon cornstarch

Place the beef in a bowl. Make a marinade by combining the soy sauce, wine, honey, ginger, and garlic, and pour it on the beef. Allow to marinate for at least half an hour, turning occasionally. Heat the oil in a large frying pan or wok (Chinese stir-frying pan) until quite hot, and add the peppers and scallions. When the peppers are slightly soft, but still bright green, remove the beef from the marinade and add it to the pan. Stir-fry over high heat until the beef starts to brown. Mix the cornstarch into the marinade, pour into the pan, and cook for another 2 or 3 minutes, until the liquid thickens slightly. Serve with plain boiled rice and beer or wine.
    Serves 4.

BEEF STROGANOFF

This mainstay of fine restaurants everywhere is claimed by both the French and the Russians. The following recipe is an adaptation, which can be prepared quickly and easily, using a large skillet or an electric frying pan.

> 1½–2 pounds lean sirloin steak
> 6 tablespoons butter
> ½ pound fresh mushrooms, sliced
> 6 scallions, chopped, or 1 onion, diced
> 3 tablespoons dry red wine
> Dash of Tabasco sauce
> Paprika
> Salt and pepper to taste
> 1 cup sour cream, at room temperature

Cut the steak into strips ½-inch thick and 2 inches long, discarding all fat. Melt 2 tablespoons of the butter in a large frying pan. Add the mushrooms and scallions and sauté over medium heat for 5 minutes. Then push vegetables to the side of the pan or remove to make room for the steak. Add the remaining butter and turn the heat up to medium-high. Add the steak when the pan is hot enough to sear the meat quickly and seal in the juices. Add the wine, Tabasco sauce, and a sprinkling of paprika. Cook, stirring frequently, for 2 to 3 minutes for rare, or about 4 minutes for medium. If you removed the mushrooms and scallions return them to the pan. Salt and pepper to taste. Then turn off the heat and stir in the sour cream. Serve immediately over buttered noodles, accompanied with a tossed green salad and French red Bordeaux.

Serves 4.

CHILI

Once a regional specialty, this honest and flavorful food has become one of America's most popular dishes, as well as an international favorite. Simple to make and extremely versatile, chili can be cooked in any large pot or skillet, in a Dutch oven or in an electric frying pan. If you brown the meat first in a frying pan, you can slow-cook chili very successfully in one of the new crock pots. Make more than you need for one meal. It can be kept in the refrigerator for several days, or frozen in individual plastic containers for later use. It is perfect for a buffet or cookout, served as the main dish of a tailgate picnic, and it is just as good when frozen and reheated in the galley kitchen of a boat. It is also popular as a sauce over grilled hamburgers and hot dogs.

Variations in chili recipes are endless. I have found, for example, that cumin adds a distinctive flavor. This spice is sometimes hard to find, but it's worth searching for. (To obtain premixed chili spices, see page 67.) Dried kidney beans, on the other hand, aren't worth the effort. Trying to be a purist, I once went though the trouble of soaking and cooking the dried beans, but found the difference was slight. Canned kidney beans are perfectly fine, as long as you drain and rinse them well, and add them toward the end of the cooking so they won't have a chance to disintegrate into the sauce. A sprinkling of sugar will counter the slightly acid taste of the tomatoes.

It is said that Texans make chili from virtually everything —venison, bear meat, possum, ground pork, or veal and beef combined. This recipe calls for chopped beef.

2 pounds chopped chuck
¼ pound bacon, cut into squares
3 onions, coarsely chopped

3 to 4 tablespoons chili powder
½ to 1 teaspoon cayenne pepper
1 tablespoon cumin
Salt and pepper to taste
1 large can (approximately 28 ounces) Italian tomatoes, packed in purée
1 6-ounce can tomato paste
½ teaspoon Worcestershire sauce
Sugar
2 medium cans of dark red kidney beans (approximately 30 to 32 ounces), drained and well rinsed
Chopped raw onion for garnish
Shredded Cheddar or Monterey Jack cheese for garnish

Form the chopped meat into teaspoon-size meatballs. They need not be perfectly round or regular. Fry the bacon pieces, starting with a cold frying pan. Remove when they are crispy. Drain on paper towels, and reserve. Add the meatballs to the pan a few at a time and fry in the bacon grease. When the meat has browned, add onions, sprinkle on the chili powder, cayenne pepper, cumin, salt, and pepper. Mix well, and then stir in the tomatoes and tomato paste. Reduce the heat to a barely bubbling simmer and cook, uncovered, for about 1 hour, stirring occasionally. Taste at this time and add the Worcestershire sauce and more cayenne pepper (if you dare). If the sauce seems too tart, add a sprinkling of sugar. Stir in the kidney beans and the reserved bacon pieces, and continue cooking only until heated through. Skim the excess fat from the surface before serving, and season to taste. Serve with chopped onions and shredded cheese to be added at the table. Cold beer and a crunchy salad are all you need to complete the meal.

Serves 4 to 6.

Variations

CUBED STEAK CHILI: When you are feeling grand, substitute tiny cubes of steak for the chopped chuck in chili. Use 2 pounds of sirloin or round steak, cut into ½-inch cubes. Follow the recipe directions, browning the steak cubes in the same manner as the chopped meat. Before adding the kidney beans and bacon, taste the meat for tenderness and cook a little longer if necessary.

CHILI CASSEROLE: An easy and practical meal to take along on a tailgate picnic or on an outing on a boat. Make the chili according to the recipe and, while still hot, turn into a heavy casserole. Prepare a package of corn bread mix and pour the batter directly over the top of the hot chili, spreading it to the edges of the casserole. Bake according to the directions on the package. The corn bread topping forms a natural cover for the chili casserole. It will hold the heat for an hour or more, and if wrapped in aluminum foil will keep even longer. The "cover" is eaten with the chili, eliminating the need to make an additional dish. Serve with a crisp salad of romaine lettuce, raw mushroom slices, and thinly sliced red onions for a perfect buffet.

CHILI AND RICE AND/OR EGGS: Serve chili over white or packaged saffron rice. Allow ½ cup of raw rice, prepared according to the package directions, per person. Another interesting idea is to serve each portion of chili topped with an egg, cooked sunny-side up.

CHILI MEXICANA: Line 4 to 6 individual casseroles or ramekins with a tortilla, quickly fried on both sides before serving with the chili. These are becoming available in more and more places, as Mexican and "Tex-Mex" food becomes increasingly popular. If you wish, top with shredded Cheddar cheese and broil quickly until the cheese melts.

HAMBURGERS

The winner and still champion. Whether they are grilled over a charcoal fire, fried, or pan-broiled, served plain and simple or in any of a variety of unconventional ways, hamburgers are the perennial favorite.

The particular type of chopped beef you use is really a matter of personal preference. To me, the chopped sirloin served in better restaurants is a bit dry, although if it is served on the rare side, it is quite flavorful. If I am really trying to impress my guests, I will mix half each of chopped sirloin and lean ground chuck. But whatever type of beef you choose, the following suggestions will help you to make the best-tasting hamburgers possible.

If you can, get the butcher to grind the meat to order for you—this way you will know that it is fresh and, if you see it before it is ground, you'll know how much fat is in it. (There are food laws about the amount of fat allowed in ground meat, but you can bet that most places will go right to the limit if they can get away with it.) Try to serve the hamburgers as soon as you can after buying the meat. Ground meat spoils far faster than regular steak, and the deterioration of flavor starts long before it becomes spoiled.

Add just a bit of liquid. Up to ¼ cup dry red wine to a pound of hamburger is very good. If you don't have any wine around, splash a bit of cold water on the meat and stir briefly with a fork. Don't add salt to the meat before cooking. It shrinks the tissues and makes for a tougher, drier burger. If you use chopped steak, you may want to mix in a little olive oil or melted butter (1 or 2 teaspoons for each burger) to compensate for the drier meat; or try putting a pat of butter on top before serving. It melts into the meat and gives it a nice juicy flavor.

There is no limit to the extra ingredients you can put into the basic hamburger. If you feel the urge, you can add bread crumbs, an egg or two, grated carrots, chopped onions, green pepper, chopped mushrooms—whatever you want. If you are feeling adventurous, try adding something a little more exotic to your hamburgers: crumbled Gorgonzola or Blue cheese, minced water chestnuts, capers, sesame seeds, currants, or chopped pecans or walnuts. The important thing to remember when making miniature meat loaves like these is that the extras should not be predominant or in large pieces. Keep everything minced and mixable with the ground meat. From time to time I like to use a quarter cup each of minced parsley and scallions—including the green tips—added to a pound of ground chuck, along with a teaspoon of Dijon mustard. The flavors meld beautifully.

Ketchup and mustard are the usual toppings for burgers, of course, but certainly not the only ones. Consider some of these classics: Worcestershire sauce, A.1. sauce; sliced onions, raw or fried in butter; hamburger relish, sliced pickles; shredded lettuce and a slice of tomato; mayonnaise; and, of course, cheese of all kinds melted on top of the burgers or on a sliced roll placed under a broiler.

Actually, you can go as far as you want. A southern friend of mine puts his favorite brand of peanut butter on top of the burger when it is done. If this one doesn't tempt you, try some of these less conventional toppings: Escoffier Sauce Robert or Sauce Diable; chopped olives; chutney; Chinese duk sauce; anchovies (see chopped steak with anchovies, page 144); pizza sauce, alone or with Mozzarella cheese melted on top; sliced eggs; grilled avocado slices; grilled mushroom slices; or sour cream and chives (at room temperature).

You can add a variety of extras to the outside as well as to the inside of your burgers. French steak au poivre (pages 135–136) can be made with ground meat instead of steak. Just press coarsely ground black pepper on top of the raw patties and fry in a mixture of butter and oil. When they are done, remove to a heated platter, turn the heat under the pan to medium, and quickly swish ⅓ cup of red wine and ½ teaspoon cornstarch into the pan, mixing with a wooden spoon to "deglaze" the pepper and meat drippings sticking to the bottom. As the sauce thickens, add salt to taste and pour over the burgers. Serve with French bread instead of the usual buns.

Whatever method you use to cook burgers, start with a hot pan or grill (unlike bacon, which should be placed in a cold pan). To pan-broil the meat, first coat the bottom of your frying pan with coarse kosher salt, get the pan very hot, and then put in the patties. This quickly sears the meat and keeps the hamburgers juicy. Don't smash them down with a spatula—leave the juices inside. To test for doneness, check them discreetly with a fork.

If you want a crusty outside, use a little olive oil in the pan—just enough to coat the bottom. It will sear the outside to retain the juices. Butter smokes at a lower temperature than oil or most types of margarine, but it does add a rich flavor, especially to chopped steak. If you want, mix half butter and half oil to keep smoking down.

CHOPPED STEAK WITH ANCHOVIES

This is an authentic French dish, which is simple and inexpensive to make. Be sure not to add salt before tasting, since the anchovies are very salty.

> 1 pound chopped chuck
> 1 2-ounce can anchovy fillets, flat or rolled with capers
> 2 tablespoons butter
> Freshly ground pepper to taste.

Divide the chopped steak into four patties. Mash 2 or 3 of the anchovy fillets with the butter, and heat in a skillet. Cook patties 3 to 5 minutes on each side in the hot skillet. Season to taste. To serve, top each patty with 3 or 4 anchovies and pour the pan juices over them. Serve with tossed green salad and cold beer.
Serves 4.

MARSHALL'S MEAT LOAF

There is a certain mystique about meat loaf. I like it, though there are people who absolutely despise this popular and practical dish. I'm sure that Freud would explain this in terms of neglected childhood, poverty, and an identification with David Copperfield! Nevertheless, the following meat loaf recipe has a lot going for it—decorative slices of eggs and stuffed olives that appear in mosaic as the loaf is cut. For extra visual interest and taste, I often add carrots, artichoke hearts, and ripe olives as well. Meat loaf also keeps well, and leftovers have a variety of uses—sliced for cold or hot sandwiches (with Cheddar or Swiss cheese melted on top), or cut up into chunks and served on crackers with cocktails. The real trick is to make the loaf in the center of a large pan and to pour off the extra fat as it comes out of the meat during cooking. It goes beautifully with plain mashed potatoes, fresh green peas and, perhaps, a loaf of crusty garlic bread (page 152).

- 2 pounds ground chuck, or 1½ pounds ground chuck and ½ pound ground lamb
- ½ cup bread crumbs
- ½ cup unsweetened wheat germ
- 2 cloves garlic, minced
- 1 tablespoon Worcestershire sauce
- 1 teaspoon Dijon mustard, or ½ teaspoon dry mustard
- 2 teaspoons salt
- 1 teaspoon freshly ground pepper
- 1 large onion, chopped
- ½ cup stuffed Spanish olives
- ½ cup grated carrots (optional)
- ½ cup drained unmarinated cooked artichoke hearts (optional)
- ½ cup pitted ripe olives (optional)
- 2 eggs, beaten
- ½ cup dry red wine or beef bouillon
- 3 hard-cooked eggs
- Parsley sprigs

Preheat the oven to 350 degrees (medium). Place all the ingredients, except the hard-cooked eggs and parsley sprigs, in a large mixing bowl. Mix thoroughly with a fork until everything is evenly distributed. Shape into an attractive loaf in a large, shallow, ungreased pan or baking dish (*not* a bread loaf pan, which will trap accumulated fat). If the loaf is crowded in the pan, place it diagonally for more room. Press the hard-cooked eggs lengthwise into the loaf, and reshape until the eggs are covered. Bake, uncovered, for about 75 to 90 minutes, until the top is brown and crusty, draining off the fat as it accumulates. Garnish with parsley sprigs before serving.

Serves 6 to 8.

FRENCH BEEF STEW À LA MARSEILLES

Here is a robust beef stew with olives for a change. Like other beef stews, it can be made in advance and tastes even better the second day. Frozen, it can be reheated on camping or boating trips.

- 3 slices bacon, cut into squares
- 3 pounds beef round or rump roast, cut into 2½-inch cubes
- 2 tablespoons olive oil
- 3 onions, chopped
- 2 cups dry red wine
- 2 cloves garlic, minced or crushed in a press
- 1 teaspoon thyme or herbes de Provence
- 1 bay leaf
- Pepper to taste
- ½ pound mushrooms, sliced
- ½ cup small stuffed Spanish olives, drained and rinsed
- Salt to taste

Fry the bacon until crisp in a heavy pan. Then drain on paper towels and reserve. Quickly braise the beef in the bacon fat until brown and seared on all sides. Remove to a platter and wash the pan. (This is necessary since the taste of the overheated fat can permeate the sauce.) Cook the onions in the olive oil at moderate heat until they are transparent, then return the beef to the pan. Add the wine, garlic, herbs, bay leaf, and pepper (but not the salt, which can make the beef tough if added too soon). Reduce the heat and simmer, covered, for 3 to 4 hours, stirring occasionally. About 15 to 20 minutes before serving, stir in the mushrooms, olives, and reserved bacon pieces. Season with salt to taste and continue simmering, uncovered, until you are ready to serve. Serve with buttered noodles or tiny new potatoes boiled in their jackets and tossed with butter and chopped parsley.

Serves 6.

CARBONNADES À LA FLAMANDE

This variation of a traditional Flemish dish can be made well in advance for a camping or boating trip or as an autumn or winter buffet dinner at home.

- 2 tablespoons oil
- 6 medium onions, coarsely chopped
- 2 garlic cloves, crushed
- 3 pounds chuck, cut into 2½-inch cubes
- ½ cup flour
- ½ teaspoon pepper
- 1 teaspoon paprika
- 1 bay leaf
- 1 teaspoon thyme
- 3 cloves
- 1 teaspoon honey
- 1 12-ounce can of beer
- Salt to taste

Heat the oil in a large heavy kettle or electric frying pan. Add the onions and garlic and cook over moderate heat, stirring occasionally, for 5 to 7 minutes, or until the onions become transparent. Trim any excess fat from the beef cubes and shake them in a paper bag, a few at a time, with the flour, pepper, and paprika. Brown the beef over high heat in the oil, adding more oil as needed, until all the cubes have been browned. Stir in the remaining ingredients except the salt. Reduce the heat, cover tightly, and simmer slowly for approximately 2 to 3 hours, or until the beef is very tender. Stir occasionally. Correct the seasoning and add salt to taste. After the beef is tender, simmer uncovered for about 15 minutes longer, to reduce the sauce. Skim off any excess fat. (If you are making the stew for later use, wait to do this until the pot cools and the fat rises to the surface.) Serve piping hot with small new potatoes boiled in their jackets, crusty French bread and, of course, beer.

Serves 6.

RUSSIAN BEEF AND CABBAGE STEW

If you have storage room, this can be prepared in advance and eaten later, or even frozen in smaller servings. This Russian stew is really a whole meal in itself. It combines the best of several old recipes, and is easily made in a large pot or in an electric frying pan. The color of the stew is a rich deep red and the unusual juxtaposition of herbs and spices makes it a memorable meal.

   3 to 4 pounds beef chuck or bottom round, cut into 2-inch cubes
   6 tablespoons salad or olive oil
   4 red onions, coarsely chopped

2 cloves garlic, minced
1 bay leaf
½ teaspoon cinnamon
1 teaspoon sugar
1 28-ounce can tomatoes, packed in purée
3 carrots, cut into 1-inch pieces
1 large red cabbage, shredded
8 ginger snaps, crumbled
2 tablespoons lemon juice
Salt and pepper to taste
1 pint sour cream, at room temperature
Fresh dill, chopped

Remove any excess fat from the beef cubes and brown in 3 tablespoons of oil over a high heat, leaving enough room around them so that the juices do not accumulate and hinder browning. Remove the beef when it is browned thoroughly, wash and dry the pan (to keep the taste of burned fat from the sauce), sauté the onions and garlic in the remaining oil over a moderate heat. Return the braised beef cubes to the pan when the onions become transparent. Add the bay leaf, cinnamon, sugar, and tomatoes. When the mixture begins to boil, reduce the heat to a gently bubbling simmer and cook, covered, for two hours, stirring occasionally. Then, stir in the carrots, cabbage, crumbled ginger snaps, and lemon juice. Cover again and simmer for another hour. Taste and season accordingly with salt and pepper. If it tastes too acidy, you may wish to add a bit more sugar. Stir thoroughly from the bottom up to blend the flavors. Simmer uncovered for another half hour to reduce the sauce. Allow the stew to "set" for 10 minutes after the heat has been turned off to amalgamate the flavors. (Like so many dishes, this tastes even better the next day, and if possible, should be made in advance.)

Serve in shallow soup bowls with a large dollop of sour cream in the center and a sprinkling of chopped fresh dill on top. (You might have to use dried dill, but fresh dill makes all the difference in the world.) Traditionally, this is served with tiny boiled new potatoes, added at the table. A simple green salad and dark pumpernickel with sweet butter make it a complete meal. Serve with a robust dry red wine—Burgundy or Chianti—or cold beer.

Serves 6 to 8.

BRAISED BEEF EN DAUBE

3 slices lean bacon
3 tablespoons olive oil
2 to 3 pounds beef round or lean chuck, cut into 2-inch cubes
3 onions (1 whole, 2 coarsely chopped)
3 cloves
4 carrots, cut into 2-inch pieces
3 stalks celery, cut into 2-inch pieces
3 tomatoes, quartered
2 cloves garlic, crushed
1 bay leaf
½ teaspoon thyme
¼ teaspoon cinnamon
¼ teaspoon ginger
10 peppercorns
1½ cups dry red wine
Salt to taste

Fry the bacon, starting with a cold pan. Remove when crisp, and set aside to drain on paper towels. Combine the olive oil with the drippings in the pan, add the beef, and brown quickly on all sides. Stick the cloves into the whole onion and add, along with all the remaining ingredients except the wine, bacon and salt. Sauté for a few minutes. Remove excess fat, then pour in the wine. Reduce the heat to a very slow simmer, and cook covered for at least 3 hours, until the meat is very tender. (If the sauce is thin, simmer uncovered until the liquid is reduced.) Just before serving, stir in the reserved bacon, and add salt to taste. Serve in a deep casserole with small potatoes boiled in their jackets or with buttered noodles.

Serves 4 to 6.

BEEF IN WINE AND MUSTARD SAUCE

My variation on a French theme with pungent Dijon mustard to give it a tangy taste.

- ⅓ cup olive oil
- 3 pounds beef chuck or round, cut into 1½-inch cubes
- 3 medium onions, chopped coarsely
- 2 cups dry red wine
- 2 tablespoons Dijon mustard (Grey Poupon is a popular brand)
- 1 bay leaf
- ½ teaspoon thyme
- ½ cup celery, cut into 1-inch pieces
- 4 medium carrots, cut into 1-inch pieces
- ½ pound fresh mushrooms, sliced (or 1 medium-size can)
- Salt and pepper to taste
- ½ cup chopped parsley

Heat 3 tablespoons of oil in a large pan or electric frying pan to a moderately high heat. Add the meat and brown quickly to seal in the juices. Allow enough room around the pieces for the liquid to cook off; brown in several stages if necessary. When the last batch has been browned, remove the beef and rinse the burned fat out of the pan. Wipe the pan with a paper towel and add the remaining oil. Add onions and cook at a moderate temperature until they are transparent. Return the meat to the pan and add the wine, mustard, bay leaf and thyme. Cover and simmer slowly for 2 hours, stirring occasionally. Stir in the celery and carrots and continue to simmer for another hour. Stir in the mushrooms and simmer, uncovered, for another half hour or until the meat is very tender. Add salt and pepper to taste. If the sauce seems too thin, raise the heat slightly for a few minutes and cook uncovered, stirring from time to time.

Sprinkle the parsley over the top just before serving. Serve with buttered egg noodles, a mixed salad, and crusty garlic bread.

Serves 6.

GARLIC BREAD

1 loaf French or Italian bread
¼ pound butter or margarine (1 stick), softened
2 or 3 cloves garlic, very finely minced or crushed in a press (if you are diffident about the garlic, use just 1 clove)

Preheat the oven to 350 degrees (or use an outdoor grill). Blend together the butter and garlic and let stand while the oven is heating (about 15 minutes). Cut the bread in 1- to 2-inch thick rounds, slicing nearly but not completely through, and spread with the garlic butter. Wrap the loaf in heavy-duty aluminum foil. Heat for 15 minutes and serve hot.

Variations

If you have no oven, separate the bread rounds and spread the top with garlic butter. Add a sprinkling of grated Parmesan cheese for variety and place under a preheated broiler (medium level, if possible) until crisp and brown.

Add 2 tablespoons of fresh chopped parsley to the butter before spreading.

13
Entrées:
Veal

These days, you have to have a truly meaningful relationship with your favorite butcher to have the slightest hope of finding the best veal. At present, it is one of the most expensive meats available and much of what looks like veal in supermarkets is really young beef. Ideally, good veal cutlets (escalopes in French, scallopine in Italian) should be similar in color to chicken breasts. They should be quite thin—approximately ¼ to ⅓ inch—and weigh about 6 ounces each. If the meat is not thin enough (less than ½ inch thick), pound it or flatten with a rolling pin. Since veal is such a delicate meat, the following recipes are generally quite simple, allowing the flavor of the meat to speak for itself, and with just a bit of sauce for interest. (If the price of veal is too steep for your budget, you can substitute turkey or chicken breast, thinly sliced and treated in the same manner.) Score lightly around the edges with a sharp knife to keep the cutlets flat while cooking.

BREADED VEAL CUTLETS

Simple veal cutlets, dipped in egg and bread crumbs, are sometimes called veal Milanese, sometimes Wiener schnitzel. By any name, they can be made with ease.

4 veal cutlets (approximately 1½ pounds), pounded thin
1 egg, beaten
1 cup Italian-style flavored bread crumbs
3 tablespoons butter
3 tablespoons light salad oil

Dip the cutlets in the beaten egg, then into a shallow bowl filled with the bread crumbs, coating both sides evenly. Heat the butter and oil in a frying pan and when it is hot, fry the cutlets over medium heat for about 6 to 8 minutes on each side, until golden brown. If they seem a bit greasy, rest them for a moment on a piece of brown paper or paper towel to absorb some of the fat. Garnish with a lemon wedge and a few sprigs of parsley. Serve with a white or light red wine, as you prefer.

Serves 4.

Variations

Top the cutlets with sautéed sliced mushrooms.

SCHNITZEL À LA HOLSTEIN: Make the cutlets as described and place a sunny-side up egg (page 118), garnished with an anchovy, on top of each cutlet.

VEAL PICCATA

This is an easy version of the classic Italian dish.

1½ pounds veal cutlets
⅓ cup flour
4 tablespoons butter
¼ cup olive oil
Juice of 2 lemons
¼ cup dry white wine or vermouth
Salt and pepper to taste
1 lemon, thinly sliced
Chopped parsley

Dredge the cutlets very lightly in the flour. Heat the butter and oil in a frying pan until quite hot, but not smoking. Quickly sauté cutlets on both sides until golden brown. Add the lemon juice and white wine, reduce the heat, and simmer for 5 minutes. Season to taste. Serve immediately, garnished with the thinly sliced lemon and parsley. Buttered noodles tossed with some toasted sesame seeds makes a nice side dish to soak up some of the delicious sauce.

Serves 4.

VEAL WITH MARSALA

This is another classic and simple dish, with the wine complementing the delicate flavor of the veal.

1½ pounds veal cutlets, pounded very thin
3 tablespoons butter
3 tablespoons olive oil
½ cup Marsala wine
Salt and pepper to taste

Dry the cutlets on a paper towel. Heat the butter and oil in a frying pan until quite hot but not smoking. Sauté the cutlets quickly—about 5 minutes on each side. Add the Marsala and stir quickly around the pan with a wooden spoon, catching the browned bits of veal in the sauce. Add salt and pepper to taste. Serve with a dry white Italian wine (Soave or Frascati) or a California Chablis.

Serves 4.

14
Entrées:
Chicken

SIMPLE ROAST CHICKEN

In many circles, this dish is the winner and still champion of fine American plain cooking. It can be as aristocratic as a crown roast of lamb or a fine fillet of beef. Plump birds of 5 pounds or more are readily available, and make an easy, satisfying, and economical meal. Add small peeled potatoes, onions, and carrots to the roasting pan about 45 minutes before the chicken is done, and you have made a complete dinner in a single pan.

Begin with a fresh large chicken with firm yellowish skin and well-developed breast. Figure at least ¾ pound of raw chicken per serving, but don't be afraid to buy an extra-large bird, because leftover chicken can be used in so many ways—and you can use the carcass for soup.

> 1 4- to 5-pound roasting chicken
> Garlic salt (optional)
> 4 tablespoons butter, softened
> Salt and pepper

Preheat the oven to 400 degrees. Wash the bird under cold running water and pat dry, inside and out, with paper towels. Sprinkle the cavity with garlic or table salt and if you wish, fill loosely with one of the stuffings that follow this recipe, closing the cavity with metal skewers or use a needle and coarse white cotton thread. Bend the wings toward the body, and tie the legs together loosely with cotton thread. Rub the skin with the softened butter and place the chicken, with the breast up, on a wire rack set in a shallow roasting pan. (Keeping the bird on a rack above the bottom of the pan will make it easier to baste.) Roast, uncovered, for about 10 minutes or until the skin becomes lightly browned. Baste the bird once with the drippings from the bottom of the pan. Then reduce the oven temperature to 325 degrees, sprinkle the bird with salt and pepper, and cover with a loose tent of aluminum foil to keep it moist. Continue spooning the pan juices over the bird frequently. After about an hour at 325 degrees, remove the tent, and continue to roast and baste until the leg joint moves easily (about 1½ to 1¾ hours for a 4-pound chicken). When pricked, the juices that come out should be clear. If the skin begins to get too dark before the chicken is done, replace the foil covering for a while, and continue to baste. My personal feeling about roast chicken and fowl in general is that it should be roasted slowly until the bird is in danger of disintegrating. When the chicken is done, place it on a heated platter and allow it to "set" for 5 or 10 minutes to make carving easier.

Serves 4.

Basic Poultry Stuffing

If you are dead set on making your own stuffing from scratch (and why not?), here is a good basic recipe for a large chicken or a small turkey—with enough left over to fill an extra pan, since there never seems to be enough stuffing to go around!

- ½ cup (1 stick) butter or margarine
- ¼ cup minced celery
- ½ cup chopped onions
- 1 chicken liver
- 6 cups stale bread, cut into cubes; or 6 cups soft bread crumbs (mix white and whole wheat for a change)
- ¼ cup minced fresh parsley
- 1 teaspoon sage
- 1 teaspoon thyme
- 1 teaspoon salt
- ½ teaspoon pepper
- ½ cup chicken bouillon or broth
- 1 or 2 eggs, beaten (optional—for a moister stuffing)

Melt the butter in a skillet, add the celery, onions, and the liver, and sauté for 5 minutes. Chop the liver. Combine all the ingredients, except the broth and eggs, in a large bowl and toss well. Then add the broth and, if you want an extra-moist stuffing, the eggs. Stir well. Pack very loosely into the cavity of the bird and close as directed. Put the extra stuffing into a pie tin or glass baking dish and bake for about 1 hour along with the chicken.

Easy Poultry Stuffings
Start with one of the packaged stuffing mixes. (They're just toasted bread cubes, tossed with the appropriate herbs—but they are convenient.) One bag or box should be more than sufficient for a good-size roasting chicken. Prepare according to the directions on the package; then consider mixing in any of the following additions (individually or in combination—it's up to you):

> 1 small can of mushroom stems and pieces
> ¼ cup finely minced onions, sautéed in butter
> ½ cup chopped celery
> Chicken liver, fried in butter and minced
> ½ cup chopped nutmeats
> ½ cup currants, raisins, or chopped dates
> 1 or 2 eggs, beaten
> 1 pint shucked oysters or clams, minced with some parsley
> 1 chopped apple
> ½ cup pitted black olives
> ¼ cup (or less) finely chopped green seedless grapes
> ½ cup chopped water chestnuts
> ¼ cup each, slivered almonds and chopped dried apricots

CHICKEN AMONTILLADO

This absolutely simple recipe has one secret: Roast the chicken at a low temperature and baste it every 15 minutes. (I know this is a bore, but it is the only way to make sure that the fragrant sherry and tarragon mixture really glazes the chicken.)

> 1 teaspoon dried tarragon, or 1 tablespoon finely chopped fresh tarragon
> 1½ cups Amontillado (medium dry sherry)
> 1 4- to 6-pound roasting chicken
> Salt and pepper
> 2 cloves garlic, finely minced

If you use dried tarragon, stir it into the sherry at least 2 or 3 hours before you are ready to make the chicken, to thoroughly flavor the wine.

Preheat the oven to 325 degrees (medium-slow heat). Wash the chicken, inside and out, under cold running water, and pat dry with paper towels. Rub the cavity with salt and sprinkle with pepper. Combine the minced garlic with the wine and tarragon mixture. Place the bird on a wire rack in a shallow baking dish or casserole. Tie the drumsticks together loosely with white cotton thread or string and tuck the wings underneath. (If the chicken is very lean, rub the skin with a little softened butter or oil—but a good roasting chicken should have enough fat under the skin to make this unnecessary.) Dribble about ⅓ cup of the sherry over the bird and place in the oven. Continue to apply the liquid at 15 minute intervals, until it is all used up. (This is one of the times a kitchen syringe is a blessing, since you can just tilt the pan a little, draw up the drippings and reapply them. If you don't have one, use a large cooking spoon.) If the bird seems to be browning too fast, cover it loosely with an aluminum foil tent. Depending on the size of the chicken, it should roast from 90 minutes to 2½ hours (20 to 25 minutes per pound). Remove the tent about 10 minutes before the chicken is done, so the color will be nice and brown. Serve with a bottle of chilled Chablis or other dry white wine.

Serves 4 to 6.

CHICKEN WITH OREGANO

1 3- to 5-pound broiling chicken, quartered
Salt and pepper
¼ cup lemon juice
Grated rind of 1 lemon
⅓ cup olive oil
2 cloves garlic, minced
1 teaspoon minced fresh parsley
2 teaspoons oregano

This classic Italian dish can be made indoors in an electric or gas broiler or barbecued out-of-doors over charcoal. Sprinkle the pieces of raw chicken with salt and pepper, and then dip them into a mixture of the lemon juice, lemon rind, olive oil, garlic, parsley, and oregano. Broil for 15 to 20 minutes on each side until browned and tender, basting occasionally with the leftover mixture. If you can catch the juices that escape, pour them over the cooked chicken. Serve with a crisp garden salad and a chilled bottle of dry Italian white wine (try Frascati or Soave).

Serves 4 to 6.

CHICKEN IN THE POT
(Poulet au Pot)

Every culture seems to have a stewed chicken and vegetable dish. This one, from France, is especially good.

1 4- to 5-pound chicken, quartered
1 teaspoon salt
Cold water
3 onions
2 leeks, quartered lengthwise
1 bay leaf
6 peppercorns
3 cloves
½ teaspoon thyme
4 carrots, cut into 3-inch pieces
4 sprigs of fresh dill
4 sprigs of fresh parsley

Put the chicken in a large pot, add the salt and cold water to cover, and bring to a boil. Reduce the heat and remove the scum as it accumulates on the surface. Add the onions, leeks, bay leaf, peppercorns, cloves, and thyme. Cover the pot and simmer gently for 1 hour. Then add the carrots, dill, and parsley, and correct the seasoning if necessary. Continue to simmer for another 30 minutes. Take the chicken out of the broth and remove the skin and bones, keeping the meat in large pieces wherever possible. Return the pieces of cooked chicken to the broth. Serve in soup bowls with buttered rounds of toasted French bread floating in the broth.

Serves 4 to 6.

ASPARAGUS AND CHICKEN MORNAY

Here is an elegant supper dish for any time you wish. Use leftover cooked chicken meat from another meal or anticipate tomorrow's dinner by adding an extra breast or 2 to the preceding poulet au pot recipe.

- 2 pounds cooked asparagus (page 196)
- 1 pound (approximately) cooked chicken, sliced into strips
- ½ pound boiled ham, sliced into thin strips
- 1 cup mornay sauce (page 82)
- ¼ cup grated Parmesan cheese
- Salt and pepper to taste

All ingredients should be warm or at room temperature before starting. Using a shallow heatproof dish, arrange the asparagus on the bottom, distributing the narrow strips of chicken and ham on top. Season the mornay sauce with additional salt and pepper if desired, and pour over the other ingredients. Sprinkle the top with Parmesan cheese. Put under a broiler until the cheesy sauce is browned and bubbly—about 5 minutes should do it, since everything is already cooked.

Serves 4 to 6.

COQ AU VIN
(Chicken in Red Wine)

One of the all-time favorites of country French cuisine, this dish is honest, flavorful, and has the distinctive richness of a red wine sauce instead of the white wine usually used with poultry. Here's a dish that can be made in advance; it also can be frozen for future use.

1 4- to 5-pound chicken, quartered or cut into smaller pieces
½ cup flour
½ teaspoon salt
½ teaspoon pepper
1 teaspoon paprika
5 tablespoons butter or margarine
2 cloves garlic, minced
⅓ cup diced ham or Canadian bacon
½ teaspoon thyme
3 cloves
1 bay leaf
1½ cups dry red wine
1 6-ounce can mushrooms, or ½ pound small fresh mushrooms
½ cup frozen pearl onions, or 12 small fresh white onions

Wash the chicken under cold running water and dry with paper towels. Put the flour, salt, pepper, and paprika into a paper or plastic bag and shake the chicken pieces one or two at a time in it until evenly coated. Melt the butter in a frying pan or skillet and sauté the garlic in it for a minute, then add the chicken pieces, and brown on both sides. Add the ham, thyme, cloves, bay leaf and red wine, and simmer, covered, over very low heat for an hour. Add the mushrooms and onions and simmer for another 20 minutes, or until tender. Taste and correct seasoning with more salt and pepper if necessary. (If the sauce is thinner than you'd like after an hour of cooking, remove the cover for a while.) Serve with the same dry red wine used in the recipe, crispy shoestring potatoes, and a mixed garden salad.

Serves 4 to 6.

CHICKEN PAPRIKA

This traditional Hungarian dish can be cooked in an electric frying pan or in a large skillet on the stove. It takes less than an hour to prepare (only 45 minutes to cook), and most of the time it can be left to simmer, while you make the rest of the dinner or entertain your guests.

> 1 3- to 5-pound frying chicken, cut into serving-size pieces
> 3 slices bacon, diced
> ½ cup flour
> ½ teaspoon salt
> ½ teaspoon black pepper
> 1 tablespoon plus 1 teaspoon paprika
> 3 tablespoons butter
> 2 onions, coarsely chopped
> 1 clove garlic, diced
> Dash cayenne pepper
> 1 cup dry white wine
> 1 cup sour cream

Rinse the chicken pieces well and dry thoroughly with paper towels. Fry the bacon quickly in a large pan, remove the pieces when they are crisp, and set aside to drain on paper towels. Combine the flour, salt, black pepper, and 1 teaspoon of the paprika in a plastic or paper bag, then shake the pieces of chicken in the bag, one by one. Transfer chicken to the bacon fat and brown on all sides, being sure to leave enough room between the pieces to allow them to brown evenly. The fat should be very hot, but not smoking. Remove the chicken pieces to a heated platter as they are browned. Discard the remaining fat and wipe the pan clean with paper towels, or wash and dry if necessary. (If this isn't done, the taste of the burned bacon fat will permeate the meat.)

Melt the butter in the pan. Add the onions, garlic, dash of cayenne pepper, and the remaining 1 tablespoon of paprika, and sauté until the onions are transparent. Then return chicken parts to the pan and add the wine. Cook over medium heat (350 degrees in your electric frying pan) until the liquid begins to boil.

Then lower the temperature to a gentle simmer, cover, and cook for 35 minutes. Add the sour cream and stir with a wooden spoon until it is thoroughly blended into the sauce. Turn up the heat again and cook, uncovered, until the sauce thickens a bit. Then stir in the reserved bacon pieces and serve immediately.

Traditionally, chicken paprika is served with broad egg noodles. Since the sauce is so rich, your vegetables should be simply steamed and served with butter and salt. You might use spinach and small baby carrots for their color as well as taste. Pearl onions also make a fine complement to this dish. Try to find Hungarian Olasz Riesling (dry white wine) or Egri Bikaver (a robust red wine, meaning "Bull's Blood") to serve with it.

Serves 4.

CURRIED CHICKEN WITH ZUCCHINI

1 onion, chopped
4 tablespoons butter or margarine
1½ to 3 tablespoons curry powder, according to taste
1 cup chicken broth
1 3- to 4-pound chicken, quartered
4 cloves
½ teaspoon grated fresh ginger, or ½ teaspoon powdered ginger
Salt and pepper to taste
2 medium zucchini, sliced in rounds
1 cup yogurt
Chutney

Sauté the onion in the butter until transparent. Add the curry powder and mix thoroughly, then add about ⅓ cup of the chicken broth, and cook over moderate heat until most of the broth has evaporated. Add the chicken and sauté until lightly browned on both sides. Reduce the heat and add the remaining chicken broth, and the cloves and ginger. Simmer for 30 minutes, or until the chicken is tender. Then season with salt and pepper to taste, and add the zucchini. Cook over low heat until the zucchini is crunchy but cooked through (about 5 to 7 minutes). Remove from the heat (or turn off your electric frying pan) and allow the curry to cool for a few minutes before stirring in the yogurt. (This keeps the yogurt from breaking down.) Serve with the chutney and with rice or noodles.

Serves 6.

BYZANTINE CHICKEN

It seems that the farther East one goes, the more inventive the seasonings become. I remember a dinner at the elegant Maison Arabe in Marrakesh, where I had a flaky pie, called pastilla, made with breast of pigeon and flavored with fragrant cinnamon. American butchers would probably throw up their hands at a request for breast of pigeon, but the following recipe for chicken with an exotic Eastern touch can be made quite easily with ingredients available anywhere.

>   3 to 4 tablespoons butter or margarine, softened
>   1 onion, minced
>   ½ cup dried apricots, soaked in warm water and chopped
>   ½ cup golden raisins or currants
>   ½ teaspoon ginger
>   ½ teaspoon cinnamon
>   ½ teaspoon mace or nutmeg
>   1 4- to 5-pound roasting chicken
>   Salt
>   ½ cup dry white wine

Preheat the oven to 375 degrees. Melt 2 tablespoons of the butter in a skillet, add the onion and sauté until transparent. Add the apricots, raisins, ginger, cinnamon, and mace, and sauté for about 3 minutes. Cool slightly. Wash the chicken under running water and pat dry, inside and out, with paper towels. Salt the cavity and fill loosely with the cooled fruit stuffing. Close the cavity with metal skewers or use a needle and coarse white cotton thread. Bend the wings toward the body, and tie the legs together loosely with cotton thread. Rub the skin with a little of the softened butter and place the chicken, with the breast up, on a wire rack set in a shallow roasting pan. Pour the wine into the pan. Roast uncovered for fifteen minutes, or until the chicken begins to brown. Then reduce the heat to 325 degrees, cover the chicken with a loose tent of aluminum foil, and continue to bake for 1½ hours, basting frequently with the juices that collect in the bottom of the pan. Serve with white or brown rice, or kasha (page 195), and white wine. A tossed salad with fresh grapefruit sections is a nice accompaniment to the spicy, fruited quality of the meal.

Serves 4.

BREAST OF CHICKEN ORIENTALE

Although this recipe uses relatively expensive boned chicken breasts, there is no waste and you can figure approximately 1½ pounds for 4 generous servings. (To economize, you can also bone the chicken breasts yourself—figure on 3 pounds of raw chicken to serve 4 generously.)

- 1 cup uncooked rice
- ½ cup cold chicken broth or water
- Dash of Tabasco or other hot pepper sauce
- ½ teaspoon cornstarch
- 2 tablespoons butter
- 2 tablespoons salad or peanut oil
- 1½ to 3 tablespoons curry powder
- 1½ pounds boned chicken breasts, cut into bite-size pieces
- ¼ cup chopped water chestnuts
- 1 10-ounce package frozen Chinese or Japanese stir-fry vegetables, or other frozen vegetables (use mushrooms, peas and pearl onions, broccoli, or French-cut green beans)
- 1 10-ounce package Chinese snow peas (optional)
- Salt to taste

Condiments
Major Grey's chutney
Pickled watermelon rind or cantaloupe
Chopped pecans
Chinese sweet-sour (duk) sauce
Coconut
Chopped hard-cooked eggs
Chopped scallions or chives

Cook the rice according to the directions on the package (it should take about 20 minutes). Since cooking time for the remaining ingredients is only about 10 minutes, start the rice ahead of time.

Combine the cold broth or water, Tabasco or other pepper sauce, and cornstarch, and set aside. Be sure the liquid is cold or the cornstarch will not blend smoothly. Heat the butter and oil in a large frying pan and add the curry powder, using 1½ tablespoons for a mild curry to 3 tablespoons for a more pronounced "hot" flavor. Add the broth mixture and the chicken pieces to the pan, and cook over high heat (400 degrees on an electric frying pan) for 4 or 5 minutes, stirring occasionally. Then add the water chestnuts and the frozen vegetables (discarding the packaged sauce mix, if any), and cook for another 2 to 3 minutes, until the vegetables are cooked but still quite crisp. Add salt to taste and serve over the cooked rice, accompanied by small dishes of any or all of the suggested condiments.

Serves 4.

BREAST OF CHICKEN WITH PISTACHIO NUTS

½ cup (1 stick) butter
2 large chicken breasts, skinned, boned and split into halves
1 clove garlic, minced

1 onion, finely chopped
½ cup sliced mushrooms
½ teaspoon thyme or herbes de Provence
1 tablespoon flour
1 cup dry white wine
2 egg yolks
½ cup heavy cream
Salt and pepper to taste
½ cup shelled pistachio nuts

Melt the butter in a large skillet and brown the chicken breasts over moderate heat until golden. Remove to a heated platter. Add the garlic, onion, and mushrooms to the skillet, and sauté for 5 minutes. Combine the thyme, flour, and wine, stir well and then add to the skillet. Cook for 3 minutes, stirring until the sauce thickens. Then return the chicken to the pan and cook in the sauce, uncovered, over low heat for another 10 to 15 minutes, until tender. Beat the egg yolks and the cream together, add a little of the hot sauce, then pour into the pan. Season with salt and pepper to taste and add the pistachio nuts. Serve with egg noodles and fresh green beans.

Serves 4.

CHICKEN LIVERS AND BACON IN WINE SAUCE

½ pound bacon, cut into 2-inch pieces
2 tablespoons butter
½ pound fresh mushrooms, sliced
1 pound chicken livers
1 teaspoon thyme or fines herbes
6 scallions, cut into ½-inch pieces
⅓ cup dry white wine
Salt and pepper to taste

Fry the bacon slowly, starting with a cold frying pan. Remove the pieces from the pan when they are crisp, drain on paper towels, and reserve. Discard the bacon grease and wipe the pan clean with paper towels. (This must be done so the taste of the burned bacon fat will not permeate the meat.) Melt the butter in the pan, add the mushrooms, and cook over medium-high heat for about 2 minutes, or until the mushrooms are tender and the juices have been evaporated from the pan. Then add the chicken livers, thyme or fines herbes, and the scallions, and cook over moderate heat for 3 more minutes, until the livers are brown. Pour the wine into the pan, reduce the heat and simmer, uncovered, for another 2 minutes. Stir in the reserved bacon pieces and salt and pepper to taste. Serve over rice or egg noodles, with spinach or zucchini as a side dish. Serve a light white wine, such as California Chardonnay or Chenin Blanc, well chilled.

    Serves 4.

15
Entrées:
Ham and Pork

CHOUCROUTE

This easy to make, flavorful Alsatian dish is based on sauerkraut, but has only the slightest resemblance to it by the time the preparations are finished. It is hearty and satisfying on a cool, crisp day, with a gutsy flavor that will appeal to all. (Don't let the sauerkraut turn you off!) For a knock-'em-dead buffet, use French Champagne instead of ordinary white wine. Refrigerate any leftovers (there probably won't be any) and reheat for dinner the next day.

- 4 thick slices of bacon
- 2 onions, sliced and separated into rings
- 2 pounds prepared sauerkraut, drained
- 12 peppercorns
- 1 bay leaf
- ½ teaspoon thyme
- 2 cloves garlic, crushed with a fork
- ½ teaspoon caraway seeds
- ¼ cup currants or raisins
- 2 cups dry white wine or champagne
- 3 pounds of meat (any combination of the following: smoked sausage links, bratwurst, Polish sausages, frankfurters, cubes of smoked pork butt or cooked country-style ham)
- 8 to 10 small boiled potatoes

Fry the bacon slowly in a large deep pan. Remove when crisp and set aside to drain on paper towels. Sauté the onions in the bacon fat, cooking until they are transparent. Add the remaining ingredients except for the meats and boiled potatoes, cover and simmer for 20 minutes. Add the meats and continue simmering, covered, for an additional 20 to 30 minutes. Stir in the reserved bacon slices. Serve with boiled potatoes and a German Moselle, beer, or even champagne.

Serves 4 to 6.

ASPARAGUS AND HAM VINAIGRETTE

2 pounds cooked asparagus (page 196)
1 pound sliced boiled ham
1 cup classic French vinaigrette dressing (page 76)
2 hard-cooked eggs
Chopped parsley

Divide the cooled cooked asparagus into 4 equal portions. Place 2 thin or 1 thick asparagus close to the edge of each slice of ham and roll up. Arrange on individual plates and cover with vinaigrette dressing. Grate the cooked eggs over the center of each serving, and decorate with parsley.

Serves 4.

PORK CHOPS ORIENTAL STYLE

8 thinly sliced center cut pork chops
1 cup Oriental sauce (page 85)
2 large onions, sliced into rings
2 to 3 tablespoons oil
1 4-ounce can water chestnuts, coarsely chopped

Marinate the pork chops in the Oriental sauce for a few hours in the refrigerator, turning occasionally. (You can add the onions to the marinade, if you wish.) Heat the oil over medium heat in a frying pan large enough to accommodate the chops in a single layer. When the oil is hot, place the chops in the pan and cook for 5 minutes on one side. Then turn over, add the onions and the marinating sauce, and cook, covered, over medium heat for approximately 20 minutes. (For hygienic reasons, pork must always be thoroughly cooked.) Sprinkle the chopped water chestnuts on top and stir through to heat them. Serve with plain boiled rice, tiny fresh peas (for a pretty color contrast), and ice cold beer or white wine.

Serves 4.

PORK MONTMORENCY

Montmorency is the French term for a dish cooked with cherries.

> 3-pound loin of pork
> 6 slices lean bacon
> 1½ cups dry red wine
> 1 cup canned pitted red cherries
> Salt and pepper to taste
> ¼ teaspoon dry mustard

Preheat the oven to 400 degrees. Lay the pork loin in a shallow ovenproof dish and arrange the bacon slices across the top. Roast for 1 hour, basting the meat every 15 minutes with a combination of the wine and ¼ cup of juice from the canned cherries. Remove the bacon and place the drained cherries along the top of the meat. (Some will slide off during the roasting, but it does not matter.) Continue to roast, basting every 15 minutes, for another hour, or until the meat releases colorless juice when pierced with a fork. (It should never be served pink.) Remove the roast, slice and arrange on a heated platter, topped with the cherries from the pan. Season the pan juice with salt and pepper to taste and add the mustard, stirring with a fork. Serve the pan juice separately, removing most of the fat from the top before bringing it to the table. You can, if you wish, serve the traditional apple sauce that often accompanies pork roasts, but try huge mushroom caps filled with fresh tiny green peas, and crispy French fries. Pork is technically a "white" meat, but any dry red or white wine will go well. Try a Spanish Rioja. Leftovers taste great the next day, served cold with lots of hot mustard.

Serves 6 to 8.

16
Entrées:
Fish and Shellfish

There is nothing more delightful than dining on fresh fish or shellfish, especially when you are within view of the waters from which they came. Fish and shellfish are both quick to fix and full of protein. The fresher they are, the better they will taste, even more so if you caught them yourself! In many parts of the country, unfortunately, fresh fish and seafood are becoming harder and harder to find, and we must contend with frozen seafood—and damned expensive at that. However, if you have a good fish market in your neighborhood, if fishing is one of your hobbies, or if your travels take you to places where commercial fishermen bring in their catches, the delights of fresh fish and shellfish are hard to exaggerate.

The delicate flavor of fish and seafood can be adapted to a veritable encyclopedia of different preparations. There are several basic and very fast ways to cook them. In my opinion, the best ways are the simplest ones: broiled over charcoal, sautéed quickly in lemon and butter, poached or boiled in a simple wine-based court bouillon, or pan-fried. These basic techniques apply to shellfish (with the shells removed first) as well as to regular fish. The cooking time for shellfish is even shorter than that for the larger, firm-fleshed fish. Serve them hot or cold, plain, or with any number of sauces.

Generally, you should allow about 8 ounces of raw fish or shelled seafood per person. Of course, you can easily adjust this according to the appetites of the diners. You can cook just about any fish or seafood according to any of these basic methods, but in each case I have suggested some types and sizes of fish that are particularly suitable. Lobster connoisseurs, for example, seem to agree that boiling is the only way to truly appreciate this aristocrat of the deep. If you buy lobster, try to buy it alive to assure freshness. Frozen lobster tails from South Africa and elsewhere are quite good, however, and are available in fish stores and supermarkets in many parts of the country, as are Alaskan king crab legs. Most recipes that call for lobster can also use crabmeat (and vice versa) or, in fact, any combination of lobster, crab, clams, and scallops. There are, by the way, two kinds of scallops: the silver-dollar-size sea scallops and the smaller and more delicate nutty bay scallops, which are better and commensurately more expensive.

FISH AND SHELLFISH SAUTÉED IN BUTTER

This method is particularly good for fillets of thin fish (small butterfly fillets of sunfish, perch, flounder, or sole), as well as for small whole fish (like smelts or trout) and almost any type of shellfish. For sautéing, I recommend butter rather than margarine, because it enhances a delicate fish like sole or flounder much more effectively than does margarine. The pan you use should be large enough so that each fillet or whole fish has room around it. If you crowd them, the juices accumulate and the fish will taste soggy.

Clean and dress the fish, and pat dry with paper towels. Sprinkle with salt and pepper. You can also dredge lightly in flour if you wish, but this is not necessary. Melt enough butter to form a generous coating on the bottom of the pan (about 3 to 4 tablespoons, depending on the size of your pan). Gently place the fish in the pan. To avoid unnecessary handling, fillets should be placed with the meaty side down first, so the skin side will be down when you serve them—be very gentle, because they break into pieces very easily. Cook uncovered over medium-high heat until lightly browned. Turn very carefully (so the skin side of the fillets is down) and cook for another minute or so. The fish cook very quickly, so be sure not to overcook. The fish are done when the flesh is opaque and flakes easily when tested with a fork. Remove to a heated platter. Add a little more butter and the juice of half a lemon to the pan, stir with a wooden spoon until well blended, and pour over the hot fish.

CHARCOAL- AND OVEN-BROILED FISH AND SHELLFISH

Because of their richness, salmon steaks or whole small trout can be barbecued beautifully, the smoke enhancing their flavor. Lobster tails or whole lobsters, split and cleaned, are delicious cooked this way, as are soft-shelled crabs and large shrimp (shelled, but with the tails left on). Large chunks of filleted fish, crabmeat or lobster, small whole shrimp or scallops can be skewered and barbecued kebob style. Of course, all fish and shellfish that do well on a barbecue are also delicious when broiled in an electric broiler or conventional stove.

If you are barbecuing, prepare the charcoal fire as you would ordinarily, making sure that the grate is 4 to 6 inches above the coals. The coals should be covered with a grayish-white ash before you place the fish on the grate. If you are cooking indoors, be sure your broiler is fully heated and the pan is 3 to 4 inches below the flame or heating coil before you start to cook.

Make a basting sauce by melting some butter (approximately 3 to 4 tablespoons per fish steak, whole fish, or portion of shellfish), adding 2 or 3 tablespoons of lemon juice or herbs, or both if you wish. To keep the fish from sticking to the grate of your barbecue grill or broiler pan, brush them first with a little of the basting sauce. Place them on the grill or in the broiler and cook for 4 or 5 minutes on one side, basting several times with the sauce. Then turn the fish and cook for 2 or 3 minutes more, again basting several times. Test with a fork for doneness: The flesh will be opaque and flake easily. Serve with a little of the extra melted butter poured over each portion.

POACHED FISH AND SHELLFISH

Poaching is a way of gently simmering fish or seafood in a liquid, usually a delicately flavored broth known as court bouillon. Almost any fish can be cooked to advantage by this method, and it is the classic way to prepare large whole fish that will be served cold. (Salmon and bass are especially good made this way, with the extra flavor and moisture that a poaching liquid can impart.)

Gourmet shops sell wonderful copper fish poachers, complete with baskets or racks for cooking a whole fish. They come in various sizes, from small enough for a trout to large enough for poaching a whole salmon or sea bass. However, these beauties cost about as much as a small fishing boat! Until you can afford such an extravagant utensil, you can make do with a conventional pan or electric frying pan, as long as it has sides high enough to be able to submerge the fish in the poaching liquid.

When preparing a fish for poaching, first wipe clean with damp paper towels. Purists insist on wrapping the fish (or fillets) to be poached in cheesecloth. This holds the fish together, it is true, but if you have too many other things to do you can eliminate this step. The fish may be a bit ragged and not as pretty when served, but it will be just as tasty.

Make a poaching liquid according to the following recipe for court bouillon. You should start to prepare this about half an hour before you begin cooking your fish. When the poaching liquid is ready, bring it to a boil. Carefully submerge the fish in the liquid, bring it back to a simmer, then lower the heat and cook gently for about 5 minutes. The time will vary with the size and flakiness of the fish; larger whole fish taking longer, of course, than small fish or fillets. The fish is done when you can flake it with a fork. Remove very carefully from the liquid with a wooden spoon. Garnish with slices of the carrots from the poaching liquid. Serve plain or with a velouté sauce made by thickening the poaching liquid (page 179).

ENTRÉES: FISH AND SHELLFISH

Poaching Liquid for Fish (Court Bouillon)

Court bouillon may sound elegantly French, but don't worry—it is very easy to make. Once the fish has been cooked in it and removed, the liquid is often known as fish stock, and can be used as the base for the velouté sauces on pages 82–83.

> 1 quart (4 cups) dry white wine
> 2 cups water
> 3 onions, sliced
> Bouquet garni (1 bay leaf, 1 teaspoon thyme, a few sprigs of parsley, tied in a piece of cheesecloth)
> 2 carrots, cut into large pieces
> ½ teaspoon peppercorns

Put all the ingredients in a large pot, cover, and cook rapidly for 30 minutes. Strain through a fine cloth or strainer before using to poach fish, or as the base for a sauce. Add salt to taste before using. Reserve the carrot pieces to use as a garnish for the poached fish. It may be frozen for future use.

BAKED FISH AND SHELLFISH

A quick and trouble-free way to cook almost any fish, baking is especially good if there are other distractions while you are preparing food. It can be timed in advance, and serving time can be scheduled more easily than with sautéing or another method of cooking which requires the undivided attention of the cook.

Clean the fish and wipe dry with a paper towel. I recommend a glass baking dish, since metal pans will sometimes affect the taste of the more delicate fish. You can marinate fish or shellfish in lemon or lime juice, or even the classic French vinaigrette (page 76) beforehand. Preheat the oven to medium hot (400 degrees). Cover the bottom of the pan with melted butter, then arrange the whole or filleted fish in the pan, dotting the top with small pats of butter. Sprinkle with salt and pepper. You may also wish to use chopped fresh dill or some paprika to add to the color. Bake uncovered for 10 to 20 minutes, depending on the size of the fish. As in other methods, the fish is done when the flesh is opaque and flakes easily with a fork. Serve the fish with lemon wedges, or with tartar sauce.

The larger fish fillets or steaks (flounder, halibut, scrod or swordfish) may be baked with a variety of sauces. Follow the preceding directions for baked fish, but after arranging the fish on the melted butter, add 1 recipe of mornay sauce (page 82), béchamel sauce (page 81), or soubise sauce (page 82). The sauce should be warm when it is poured onto the fish; then bake as usual.

FRIED FISH

This method is best suited to small whole fish and fillets of manageable size. Allow about ⅓ to ½ pound of raw fish per person. To bread, dip the fish in 2 beaten eggs, then roll in about a cup of flavored bread crumbs or crushed corn flakes. Heat butter in a large frying pan to a moderate heat but do not allow it to smoke, and fry uncovered until golden brown and crisp (about 3 to 4 minutes on each side). Be sure to turn carefully with a spatula. Serve with lemon wedges and/or tartar sauce (page 80).

SESAME FISH ROULADES

This simple and handsome dish is the ideal solution to the problem of preparing a fish dinner for a large number of people without having to prepare it in stages. The special touch of sesame seeds adds a delicate flavor and delicate texture difference to the fish. You may use fillets of sole, flounder or scrod—or any other medium-size fish fillets. Allow ⅓ to ½ pound of fish per person, depending on appetites and what else you are serving. This is particularly suited to an electric frying pan.

    2 to 3 pounds of fish fillets
    1 teaspoon salt

1 teaspoon thyme or fines herbes
½ teaspoon white or black pepper
¼ cup (2 ounces) sesame seeds
4 tablespoons butter
1½ cups dry white wine or champagne
Chopped fresh dill or parsley (for garnish)

Cut each fillet lengthwise into two pieces and rinse in cold water, patting dry on paper towels. Arrange skin-side down on wax paper. Sprinkle with salt, pepper, herbs, and then coat evenly with all the sesame seeds. Carefully roll the split fillets into spirals with the sesame seeds inside, fastening each securely with a toothpick. Melt the butter in a large frying pan and arrange the fillets in the pan with a little space around each. Pour in the wine and bring it to a boil. Immediately reduce the heat to a gentle simmer and cover, after spooning a bit of the wine mixture into the center of each roulade. After 5 minutes, test for doneness with a fork (the fish should be opaque and flake easily). Do not overcook. Remove gently to a heated platter with a slotted spoon or spatula and pour the liquid over the fish. Sprinkle with chopped dill or parsley.

The ideal accompaniment to this dish is a fresh green vegetable—spinach or green beans—and rice, with the sauce poured on it.

Serves 4 to 6.

SAUTÉED FISH THEODORA

I made up the name because it was created at a friend's house one night when these were the only ingredients at hand. You can use any fillet of fish—flounder, sole, haddock, halibut, cod. The relatively unorthodox use of red wine makes the fish more pungent, less delicate than the more usual white wine. Figure about ⅓ to ½ pound of raw fish per person. This recipe will serve 4, but can be increased proportionally. It is also a good way to use leftover wine from another meal!

2 pounds fish fillets
4 tablespoons butter
2 to 3 ripe tomatoes
1 green pepper
1 large onion
½ bunch scallions
1 teaspoon thyme leaves
1 teaspoon salt, or to taste
Freshly ground pepper
1½ cups dry red wine
Minced fresh parsley

Rinse the fillets under cold water and pat dry with paper towels. Melt the butter in a large frying pan over medium heat (or electric frying pan at 300 degrees). Coarsely chop the tomatoes, pepper, onion, and scallions (including the green tops) and sauté for 3 minutes, stirring occasionally. Sprinkle the thyme, salt, and pepper on the vegetable mixture, add ½ cup of the wine, and stir. Add the fish, skin-side up, and cook over moderate heat for 3 to 4 minutes, then turn over gently with a spatula, trying to keep the fillets intact. Push the vegetables aside so the fish touch the bottom of the pan, and lower the heat slightly. Pour in the remaining wine gradually as the fish cooks. (This is to make a rich sauce without boiling the fish.) Test the fish for doneness after about 5 minutes—if it is ready, the flesh will flake when touched with a fork. Fillets of sole or flounder will be done faster than cod or halibut. Transfer carefully to a heated platter, sprinkle with the fresh parsley, and serve immediately. (If you wish, you can *always* serve lemon wedges with any kind of seafood.) Serve with a light dry red wine—perhaps an Italian Bardolino, a French Beaujolais, or a California Pinot Noir.

SALMON CROQUETTES

1 15½-ounce can red salmon
1 cup Italian-style flavored bread crumbs
1 onion, finely chopped
½ cup diced green pepper
2 carrots, finely shredded
3 eggs, beaten
¼ cup chopped green or black olives
3 tablespoons chopped fresh parsley
1 teaspoon fresh dill or ½ teaspoon dried dill
4 to 6 tablespoons butter
Lemon wedges

Put the canned salmon, including any liquid, in a mixing bowl. Remove the skin and the larger bones. Add ½ cup of the bread crumbs, onions, carrots, green pepper, eggs, olives, parsley, and dill, and mix until thoroughly blended. Form the mixture into patties about 3 to 4 inches in diameter and ¾ to 1 inch thick. Roll the patties in the remaining bread crumbs. Melt the butter in a skillet or electric frying pan, add the salmon patties. Fry over medium heat for approximately 4 minutes, turn, and fry for another 3 minutes until brown on both sides. Serve very hot with the lemon wedges. Serve horseradish mayonnaise (page 81) on the side, if desired. For dinner, salmon croquettes may be served with buttered noodles and fresh Lima beans, accompanied by a chilled bottle of Chablis or other dry white wine. Leftovers are excellent the next day, served cold as an appetizer.

Serves 4.

SCAMPI
(Broiled Shrimp, Italian Style)

2 pounds large raw shrimp, shelled and cleaned
1 cup olive oil
1 tablespoon lemon juice
2 cloves garlic, minced
½ teaspoon salt
¼ teaspoon cayenne pepper
2 tablespoons chopped fresh parsley
Lemon wedges

Preheat broiler. Rinse the shelled raw shrimp in cold water, dry with paper towels, and arrange in a shallow broiling pan. (A shallow heatproof baking dish that can be brought to the table will eliminate one more serving dish to be washed.) Mix together the oil, lemon juice, garlic, salt, and cayenne pepper, and pour over the shrimp. Broil 4 to 5 inches below the broiler for 2 to 3 minutes, turn and broil on the other side for 2 minutes, basting with the sauce that collects in the pan. Sprinkle parsley over the shrimp, accompany each portion with a wedge of lemon, and serve on rice.

Serves 4 to 6.

SHELLFISH DE JONGHE

½ cup butter (1 stick) softened
2 cups bread crumbs
1 clove garlic, minced
3 scallions, including the green tops, finely minced
¼ cup dry sherry
2 tablespoons lemon juice
¼ teaspoon freshly grated nutmeg
½ teaspoon fresh tarragon leaves, or ¼ teaspoon dried tarragon
2 pounds raw shrimp or other shellfish, shelled and cleaned
1 tablespoon chopped parsley

Preheat oven to 375 degrees. Heat the butter in a skillet or electric frying pan and stir-fry the bread crumbs until they begin to brown. Add the garlic, scallions, sherry, lemon juice, nutmeg, and tarragon, mixing well. Layer the shrimp and the crumb mixture in a shallow baking dish or in individual ramekins, topping with a layer of the bread crumbs. Bake for 20 minutes, or until the crumb topping is well browned.

Serve 4 to 6.

CURRIED SHELLFISH

This attractive dish can be served in a chafing dish, and is equally good for a buffet dinner or for a tailgate picnic.

- 1 pound raw shellfish, shelled and cleaned (use shrimp, crabmeat, or lobster meat, or any combination)
- ½ cup (1 stick) butter or margarine
- ½ cup chopped onions
- 1 tablespoon hot curry powder, or more to taste
- 1 clove garlic, minced
- ½ teaspoon freshly grated ginger, or ¼ teaspoon dry ginger
- 3 tablespoons flour
- 1 tablespoon lemon juice
- 1 tablespoon grated lemon rind
- 1½ cups light cream or half-and-half
- ½ teaspoon salt
- 3 dashes hot pepper sauce or Tabasco sauce
- ¼ cup Major Grey's chutney
- ½ cup drained mandarin orange sections
- Shredded coconut, chopped peanuts, pickled watermelon rind, chopped egg (for garnish)

Boil the shellfish in salted water just until they turn pink. Drain and reserve. Melt the butter in a frying pan or chafing dish, and sauté the onions until transparent. Add the curry powder, garlic, ginger, and flour, stirring as it heats until bubbly. Remove from (or turn down) the heat as you slowly stir in the lemon juice, rind, cream, salt, and pepper sauce. Add the chutney, cooking over moderate heat until thickened, stirring constantly. Stir in the shellfish, cooking only until heated through. Stir in the mandarin orange sections just before serving. Garnish with any or all of the condiments, and serve with white rice.

Serves 4.

SZECHWAN SEAFOOD

This delicious Chinese dish can be made with either shrimp, lobster, or crabmeat, or any combination—they actually enhance one another when intermixed.

- 2 pounds fresh or frozen shellfish, shelled and cleaned (use shrimp, crabmeat, or lobster, or any combination)
- Sesame or peanut oil
- 1 bunch scallions, including the green tops, cut into ½-inch pieces
- 1 clove garlic, minced
- 1 cup (approximately) Oriental sauce (page 85)
- ¾ cup chili sauce
- ¼ to ½ teaspoon hot red pepper or Szechwan pepper
- 1 tablespoon freshly grated fresh ginger or 1 teaspoon dry ginger
- Chopped peanuts (optional)

If you are using frozen shellfish, thaw to room temperature. Heat enough oil to cover the bottom of your electric frying pan or wok. Add the shellfish, a few at a time, cook over medium-high heat, turning frequently until they turn pink (about 3 minutes). As they are done, remove to a heated platter. Add the scallions and garlic to the pan, along with another tablespoon or 2 of oil. Stir-fry, using a wooden spoon, for 3 to 4 minutes. Then add all the remaining ingredients, except for the shrimp and peanuts, and cook for 5 minutes, stirring frequently. Return the shrimp to the pan and cook only until they are heated through and covered with sauce. Garnish with chopped peanuts, if you wish, and serve with boiled rice.

By the way, be prepared with plenty of ice cold beer to put out the fire of this spicy dish.

Serves 6.

17

Entrées:

Pasta and Grains

PASTA WITH WHITE CLAM SAUCE

I say pasta rather than spaghetti because I really prefer enriched linguine to spaghetti. This is an easy dish to prepare—at home, on a boat, or in a camper. For a different touch, try green (spinach) linguine or spaghetti.

>   2 to 3 cloves garlic, minced
>   ⅔ cup olive oil
>   1 10-ounce can minced clams, in broth
>   ¼ cup minced fresh parsley
>   Salt and pepper to taste
>   1 pound pasta (thin linguine or spaghetti)

Combine the garlic and olive oil in a saucepan and heat for a minute or so, but do not brown. Add the clams, including the broth, 1 tablespoon of the parsley, and salt and pepper to taste. Cook, covered, over low heat for 5 minutes. While the sauce is simmering, cook the pasta in rapidly boiling salted water, according to the directions on the package. (Add 1 tablespoon of oil to the water to keep the pasta from sticking together.) Don't overcook—the pasta should be al dente, firm to the bite. Drain well. To serve, sprinkle the remaining parsley over the pasta, pour on the sauce, and toss with 2 forks.

   Serves 4.

FETTUCCINE ALFREDO

With compliments to Alfredo, this Roman recipe is guaranteed to be delicious—and deliciously fattening. It is simple to make anywhere if you have a way to boil water, and is certain to be a real crowd-pleaser. Serve it with a mixed green salad of crunchy romaine or chicory and other garden greens, perhaps with a few very thin slices of mild red onion tossed in as an extra touch. The salad dressing should be a simple one of oil and wine vinegar to contrast with the richness of the creamy sauce.

- 1 pound fettuccine noodles
- ½ cup (1 stick) butter, softened
- ½ cup heavy cream
- ½ cup freshly grated Parmesan cheese (with additional cheese for passing at the table)
- Freshly ground black pepper

Cook the fettuccine in boiling salted water, according to the directions on the package, until they are al dente—firm to the bite. While the noodles are cooking, prepare the sauce. Using a wooden spoon, beat the softened butter, adding the cream a little at a time until light and fluffy. Gradually add the grated cheese, blending it in thoroughly. Set aside. When the fettuccine is cooked, drain it thoroughly and turn into a heated serving bowl. Add the sauce and toss with 2 forks (wooden ones, if possible), lifting it high to make sure all the pasta is coated. Serve immediately, with lots of freshly ground pepper and extra Parmesan cheese. (I like to pass a hunk of Parmesan cheese and an old-fashioned grater around the table so my guests can grate their own cheese.)

Serves 4.

LASAGNA

This Italian favorite is perfect for picnics or buffets. It is hearty, can be made ahead of time, and it takes to the freezer like a polar bear! It can be a pain in the neck to make, but is well worth the trouble (the worst part is assembling all the ingredients).

½ cup olive oil

2 onions, chopped

2 pounds ground chuck, or 1 pound ground chuck and 1 pound sweet Italian sausage

2 cloves garlic, minced

1 quart classic Italian tomato sauce (page 192), or your favorite commercially prepared tomato, mushroom, or meat sauce

1 teaspoon salt

½ teaspoon freshly ground black pepper

1 teaspoon chopped fresh basil, or ½ teaspoon dried basil

½ teaspoon oregano

1 teaspoon sugar (optional)

1 pound lasagna noodles (buy green [spinach] lasagna noodles, if you can find them)

1 pound Ricotta cheese

1 cup grated Parmesan cheese

1 pound Mozzarella cheese, chopped

¼ cup chopped fresh parsley, or 2 tablespoons dried parsley

Heat the oil in a large skillet, add the onions and sauté until transparent. Form the ground beef (and sausage meat, if you use it) into small balls (about the size of walnuts) and cook until brown, adding the garlic as the meat cooks. Then add the tomato sauce, salt, and pepper. Taste the sauce and, if you're using commercially prepared sauce and it is too bland for you, add basil and oregano. Simmer very slowly for 1 hour or more, stirring frequently. If the sauce tastes sharp, the teaspoon of sugar will reduce the acidity.

When the sauce is nearly done, preheat the oven to 350 degrees. Cook the lasagna noodles according to the directions on the box, adding 1 or 2 tablespoons of oil to the water to keep them from sticking. Rinse in cold running water and drain very well. Butter a large shallow baking dish or roasting pan and arrange alternating layers of sauce, noodles, meat, and cheese, sprinkling the parsley on top of the cheese. Pour the remainder of the sauce on the top and sprinkle with Parmesan and a few pieces of the mozzarella. Bake for 30 to 45 minutes, until the lasagna becomes bubbly and slightly browned. You can freeze the lasagna for later use. Thaw it completely before putting it into the oven. Serve with a crisp romaine or mixed green salad, garlic bread (page 152), and Italian Chianti or Valpolicella.

Serves 8 to 10.

RAVIOLI WITH LEMON AND BUTTER

Quite frankly, anyone without a spacious kitchen (and the patience of an Italian saint) will not try to make ravioli from scratch. Making the pasta itself isn't all that difficult, but once you're done, you still have to prepare the cooked chopped meat or cheese, and fill each little pocket of pasta dough. All this takes a great deal of time, even with a practiced hand. However, frozen ravioli (not the soggy canned variety) is available in many supermarkets. Purists may shudder at this advice, but if you really like ravioli and can't get it together to make it yourself, frozen ravioli can be quite respectable. Be sure to buy plain meat or cheese ravioli, without any sauce. This simple lemon and butter sauce is delicious on ravioli or, for that matter, on any filled or unfilled pasta.

1 pound frozen meat- or cheese-filled ravioli, without sauce
4 tablespoons butter
1 clove garlic, minced
Juice of 2 lemons
Grated rind of 2 lemons
¼ cup chopped fresh parsley
½ to ⅔ cup grated Parmesan cheese
Salt and pepper to taste.

Cook the ravioli according to the package directions. While it is cooking, melt the butter in a small saucepan, add the garlic, and sauté over low heat for a minute or so. Stir in the lemon juice, grated rind, and parsley. When the ravioli is done, drain well and return to the pot. Add the butter sauce, tossing to coat all the ravioli. Add the cheese gradually, until well distributed. Season with salt and pepper to taste.

Serves 4.

CLASSIC ITALIAN TOMATO SAUCE

This is a simple version that has an entire library of variations. Cooking time can vary, and a slow cooker works very well—if you have the time. If you are cooking for a crowd, the recipe can be doubled or tripled with perfect results.

- 2 to 3 tablespoons olive oil
- 2 cloves garlic, minced
- ½ cup chopped onions
- 1 28-ounce can Italian tomatoes, undrained; or 3½ cups fresh Italian plum tomatoes, cut into pieces
- 1 6-ounce can tomato paste
- 1 teaspoon dried basil, or 1 tablespoon minced fresh basil
- 1 teaspoon oregano
- 1 teaspoon sugar
- 1 teaspoon salt
- Freshly ground pepper to taste
- ¼ cup grated Parmesan cheese

Heat the olive oil in a large pan, adding the minced garlic for a robust Neapolitan flavor (if not, omit the garlic). Add the onions, and sauté over moderate heat until transparent. Add the tomatoes (if you use canned tomatoes, do not drain them), tomato paste, basil, oregano, sugar, salt, and pepper. Reduce the heat to a very slow simmer and cook, covered (but with the cover slightly ajar), for about 1 hour, stirring occasionally. Correct the seasonings and add the Parmesan cheese. If you want a more concen-

ENTRÉES: PASTA AND GRAINS

trated sauce, uncover the pan and continue cooking, very slowly, stirring frequently, until the sauce is as thick and rich as you want.

Serves 4.

Variations

Ground beef, meat balls, sweet or hot Italian sausages, clams, or other shellfish can be added to the basic tomato sauce. Use ½ pound, or more if you wish. Seafood and cooked meats should be added about 5 minutes or so before the sauce is done. If you wish to cook meats along with the sauce, brown them first in the pan with the onions, and continue cooking with the other ingredients.

PESTO SAUCE FOR PASTA

This elegant Italian sauce for pasta is as simple to make as it is delicious. It absolutely requires fresh basil—there is no getting around it. However, you can make pesto when you can find the fresh herb and freeze small containers of it for later use. Try using it on fresh pasta if you can find it—or if you want to make it yourself. It also does well on rice and green spinach noodles. Use a blender to combine ingredients or, even better, an old-fashioned mortar and pestle.

- 2 cups fresh basil leaves
- 3 cloves garlic
- ½ cup pignole (pine) nuts or walnuts
- 1 cup freshly grated Parmesan cheese (or mixture of Parmesan and Romano)
- ½ teaspoon salt
- 1 cup olive oil

If you use a blender, add half the dry ingredients, turn on to a low speed, and trickle in half the olive oil, blending until you make a thick paste with the consistency of sour cream. Remove from the blender and repeat with the remaining half of the ingredients. In a mortar and pestle, work the ingredients into a smooth paste, trickling in the olive oil a little at a time.

Serves 4 on pasta.

CHINESE FRIED RICE

Fried rice is one of those magical dishes that combines virtually everything but the kitchen sink in a wonderful medley of flavors and textures. Make it if you are having a weekend away somewhere and want to make a quick getaway on Sunday. It always seems a pity to throw food away at the end of a stay—and fried rice can eliminate such problems. All you need to do is use rice the night before instead of potatoes or noodles, make enough extra for the following day's fried rice, and you are on your way. Use chopped cooked pork, beef, chicken, ham, shrimp—any leftovers you have around. You can use almost anything under the sun without fear.

> ½ cup sesame or peanut oil
> Minced garlic (optional)
> ½ cup chopped scallions, including the green tops
> ½ teaspoon freshly grated ginger, or ½ teaspoon dried ginger
> 4 cups cold cooked rice
> ¼ cup soy sauce, or more to taste
> 1 teaspoon honey
> ¼ cup chopped water chestnuts
> ½ cup bean sprouts
> 1 cup diced cooked meat (pork, beef, chicken, ham, shrimp, or any combination of them)
> 2 eggs, beaten
> Chopped almonds or pecans (for garnish)

Heat the oil (and a hint of garlic, if you wish) in a large electric frying pan or, ideally, a wok. When it is hot, add the chopped scallions and ginger, and cook for about a minute, stirring constantly with a wooden spoon or spatula. Then add the cooked rice, pressing it down with the spoon to distribute it evenly as it cooks. Mix the honey with the soy sauce, pouring it on the rice as it heats. As you stir, add the rest of the ingredients, except the beaten eggs and the garnishes. When everything is heated through, push the rice aside to make a small space in the center. Drop the beaten egg into this pocket, and when it begins to congeal, take a fork and pull the cooked egg out of the center and onto the hot rice. When nearly cooked, use the wooden spoon to stir everything through with a tossing motion. Serve garnished with chopped almonds or pecans. It makes an interesting supper entrée or a side dish with shellfish or plain meat.

Serves 4 as an entrée; or 6 as a side dish.

KASHA (BUCKWHEAT GROATS)

This unusual grain can be served as a side dish instead of potatoes or rice. It can be made easily in a skillet or electric frying pan and has the added advantage of being very wholesome and full of all sorts of natural nutrients. Leftover kasha can be combined with egg noodles to make kasha varnishkes (below).

 2 cups kasha (buckwheat groats)
 2 eggs, beaten
 6 tablespoons rendered chicken fat, melted butter, or margarine
 4 cups chicken or beef broth, heated
 ½ teaspoon salt

Mix together the kasha and the beaten eggs. Melt the chicken fat or butter in a frying pan over high heat. Add the kasha and egg mixture to the hot pan, stirring constantly. When the kasha grains are separate and dry, pour in the hot broth, add the salt, and stir thoroughly. Turn the heat down and simmer, covered, for 30 minutes without stirring, or until all of the liquid has been absorbed. Taste and correct the seasoning. Toss with a fork to separate the grains and serve.

Serves 6 to 8.

KASHA VARNISHKES

Mix 1 cup of cooked kasha with 2 cups of hot cooked egg noodles. The noodles traditionally used are "bow ties," but any good egg noodle will do. Toss with 2 or 3 tablespoons of butter and serve.

Serves 4 to 6.

18
Vegetables

ASPARAGUS

These elegant beauties have been prized since ancient days and for good reason. There is nothing as delicious as the first tender asparagus of the season, tender and delicate. In Europe, white asparagus are prized, and only the very tips are eaten, which seems like the height of extravagance to me. The very chic eat them with their fingers, which stopped me dead in my tracks the first time I saw it at the Ritz in Paris, but I figured they knew what they were doing—so, if you like to eat with your fingers, here's your chance!

They are delicious even when cooked in the simplest way, and can be used as the base for a variety of side dishes, appetizers, and entrées. A pound of asparagus will serve 4 as a side dish or appetizer. or 3 as a lunch or dinner entrée.

To prepare, first cut off the tough white part just where it begins to turn green—or snap off with your fingers. Scrub the asparagus clean with a stiff brush, under running water. Place them whole in a large pan or heatproof dish and cover with cold water. Add ½ teaspoon salt, cover, and boil gently for about 5 to 7 minutes, or until they are tender when pricked with a fork. Serve with melted butter and a squeeze of lemon juice.

Asparagus Vinaigrette

1 pound cooked asparagus
1 cup classic French vinaigrette dressing (page 76)
Pimientos (optional)

Place the cooked asparagus in a long shallow serving dish and cover with the vinaigrette dressing. Allow them to marinate for 1 to 2 hours before bringing them to the table, decorated with strips of pimiento.

Serves 4.

"CRUMBY" GREEN BEANS

1 pound fresh green beans or 2 10-ounce packages
  frozen French-style green beans
2 tablespoons butter or margarine
4 tablespoons Italian-style flavored bread crumbs
Salt and pepper to taste

If you use fresh beans, snap off the ends and cut into diagonal pieces. Cook in a cup of salted water, covered, for 6 to 7 minutes, or until just tender. (Frozen beans should be prepared according to package directions.) Melt the butter in a saucepan and add the bread crumbs. Cook over medium heat, stirring constantly, until the crumbs are toasty brown. Drain the beans well, and toss in the saucepan with the crumbs until well coated. Serve at once.

Serves 4.

CARROTS WITH DILL

1 pound fresh carrots
2 tablespoons butter
2 to 3 tablespoons fresh dill, finely chopped
Salt and pepper to taste

Wash and scrape the carrots and cut into uniform rounds. Barely cover with salted water, and boil gently until just tender. Drain very well and toss with the butter and dill. Season with salt and pepper to taste.

Serves 4 to 6.

Variation

Emphasize the natural sweetness of the carrots by adding a tablespoon of honey or brown sugar to the drained carrots, substituting chopped fresh parsley for the dill.

CAULIFLOWER WITH BROWN BUTTER

1 large head of cauliflower
4 tablespoons butter
2 teaspoons lemon juice
Freshly ground nutmeg (optional)
1 tablespoon capers, drained

Steam the cauliflower, whole, in a tightly covered pot until just tender (about 10 to 12 minutes). Keep the lid on the pot tightly before checking; or, if preferred, cut the head into flowerets and steam for 8 to 10 minutes. Check for tenderness. Remove from heat and drain well. While the vegetable is cooking, slowly heat the butter in a saucepan until it turns nut brown. Stir in the lemon juice and nutmeg, then drizzle on the cooked cauliflower, arranging the capers on top as a garnish.

Serves 4.

BRAISED ENDIVE

Belgian (sometimes called French) endive is the aristocrat of the salad greens—it is expensive, but has a subtle, slightly bitter taste that is unique. (I understand that Belgian endive is actually chicory, but grown differently.) Once you get over the shock of paying about the same for a vegetable that you would for a decent pound of meat, this recipe is worth it, and for more than culinary one-upsmanship!

2 pounds fresh Belgian endive
4 tablespoons butter
Salt and pepper to taste

Wash the endive, wipe dry with paper towels, and cut them into quarters, lengthwise. Melt the butter in a heavy pan, add the endive, and cook gently for half an hour. Season with salt and pepper to taste.

Serves 4 to 6.

STUFFED MUSHROOMS

When your local green grocer or supermarket has those great big mushroom caps that look like something out of *The Wizard of Oz,* take the opportunity to make stuffed mushrooms. As a side dish or appetizer, figure about 4 servings to a pound of mushrooms—perhaps 2 servings to a pound as a supper entrée. Mushrooms contain almost no calories whatsoever, so if you're on a diet, you can nibble on raw mushrooms as a snack. Unfortunately, all the wonderful ways of fixing them use fattening things, so what you lose on the mushrooms you gain on the butter, cheese, and other goodies.

Once more, if you are out in the wild and find mushrooms that look good, restrain yourself—even seasoned food foragers can't always tell the deadly from the edible ones.

1 pound large fresh mushrooms
4 tablespoons butter
1 clove garlic, minced
½ cup Italian-style flavored bread crumbs
¼ teaspoon nutmeg
Salt and pepper to taste
¼ cup chopped fresh parsley

Wipe the mushrooms clean with damp paper towels (washing them in water makes them soggy). Break off the stems, trim away the very ends, and mince the stems finely. Melt 3 tablespoons of the butter in a frying pan, add the minced stems and the garlic, and sauté for 3 minutes. Add the bread crumbs, nutmeg, and salt and pepper to taste. Remove from pan and reserve. Melt the remaining butter and add the mushroom caps. Cover and sauté over low heat for 5 minutes. Carefully arrange the cooked mushroom caps on a sheet of foil or baking dish, filling each with a rounded spoonful of the filling. Place under a preheated broiler just until the tops are toasty, and sprinkle with chopped parsley before serving.

Serves 4 as an appetizer, or 2 as a luncheon or supper entrée.

Variations
Put a tiny shrimp on top of each before broiling.
Sprinkle Parmesan cheese on the top of the stuffing before broiling.
Mix 4 tablespoons of canned minced clams with the stuffing before sautéing the bread crumbs.

SAUTÉED MUSHROOMS

1 pound fresh mushrooms
4 tablespoons butter
1 tablespoon minced onion (optional)
Salt and pepper to taste

Wipe the mushrooms clean with damp paper towels and trim away the very ends of the stems. Slice them, stems and all, lengthwise. Melt the butter in a frying pan and sauté the onion until transparent. If you do not wish to use onion, simply put the mushrooms into the melted butter, and sauté for 3 to 5 minutes. Season with salt and pepper to taste. Serve on toast points.

Serves 4.

RATATOUILLE
(Vegetable Stew)

This fragrant vegetable stew is the essence of provincial French cooking. It can be served as a hot or cold vegetable dish with roast meat or chicken, as a cold appetizer, or as a filling for crepes. Make it in summer, when local produce is fresh and ripe.

2 pounds eggplant, unpeeled and cut into 2-inch cubes
3 pounds ripe tomatoes, cut into chunks
2 pounds zucchini, or 1 pound summer squash and 1 pound zucchini, sliced in rounds
½ cup chopped fresh parsley
1 pound green peppers, cut into chunks or strips
1 pound onions, sliced thin
2 to 3 cloves garlic, minced
1½ cups olive oil
½ teaspoon salt
Pepper to taste
1 teaspoon thyme, or ½ teaspoon basil and ½ teaspoon thyme
1 tablespoon capers (for garnish)

Heat the oil in a heavy pan, add the garlic and onions, and cook until the onions are just transparent. Add all the other vegetables, sprinkling on the herbs and the salt and pepper as you arrange the vegetables. Cook, covered, for about 20 minutes over medium heat, carefully stirring from time to time to avoid burning. Then reduce the heat to a very slow simmer and cook, uncovered, for another 15 minutes to evaporate excess liquids. The sauce should be thick and concentrated. Serve warm with oven-heated French bread; or chill and serve as an appetizer. (It keeps well in the refrigerator.) When serving cold, add capers, if desired.

Serves 10.

ITALIAN-STYLE SPINACH

1 pound fresh spinach
3 tablespoons olive oil
2 cloves garlic, minced
Salt and pepper to taste

Wash (and wash and wash) the spinach under running water to remove as much sand as possible. Break off the stems and discard, along with any leaves that look tired or wilted. Shake dry in a colander or wire basket. Heat the oil in the bottom of a pan large enough to accommodate the spinach without too much crowding. Fry the minced garlic in the oil for a minute or 2 over high heat and add the spinach. Cover tightly, reducing the heat to medium, and cook for 3 minutes. Check for doneness and cook a little longer, if necessary (it should still be dark green). Season with salt and pepper to taste. Serve immediately.

Serves 3 to 4.

Variation
Omit the garlic and use butter and ½ teaspoon of nutmeg instead of oil. You can also garnish with a chopped hard-cooked egg, and toss just before serving.

ACORN SQUASH

This decorative dark green vegetable is full of vitamins and can be cooked in a variety of simple ways. One of the best is to cut the squash in half and place, with the cut sides down, in a shallow baking dish. Add ½ cup water, bake in a 350-degree oven for 45 minutes to 1 hour. Serve with grated nutmeg and lots of butter. If you want, also sprinkle a teaspoon of brown sugar on the hot squash before serving.

Serves 2.

ZUCCHINI ORIENTAL STYLE

An unusual side dish, in which sesame seeds add an interesting texture and nutty flavor as counterpoint to the crunchy zucchini.

 4 or 5 medium zucchini (or summer squash)
 ½ cup soy sauce
 ¼ cup white wine
 1 teaspoon dry ginger
 1 clove garlic, minced

½ teaspoon cornstarch
1 tablespoon honey
3 tablespoons light salad oil (peanut or corn oil)
3 tablespoons sesame seeds

Trim ends from zucchini and slice lengthwise into quarters. Cut across into 3-inch pieces. Combine all the other ingredients except oil and sesame seeds in a mixing bowl and stir well, making sure the honey is dissolved. Heat the oil over medium heat in a wok or the largest frying pan you have, and arrange the zucchini so they will cook evenly. Add the liquid and simmer slowly, uncovered, for about 6 minutes. Just before serving, sprinkle the sesame seeds over the top. Serve with broiled chicken or with any Japanese or Chinese meal.

Serves 4 to 6.

19
Desserts

FRUIT COBBLER

Preparing a fruit cobbler is so easy that anyone can make it. If you don't have a regular oven, check the directions on your electric frying pan or other appliance to see if it can be adapted for baking. The cobbler can be put together in no time at all and works equally well with a variety of fresh or canned fruit. However, if the fruit you use is super-juicy, you may have to bake it a bit longer. Do not use pie-filling fruits, since they are packed in heavy syrup.

> ¼ pound butter or margarine (1 stick)
> 1 cup flour
> 1 cup sugar
> 2 teaspoons baking powder
> ¾ cup milk (or buttermilk)
> Pinch of salt
> 3 to 4 cups fruit (apples, apricots, peaches, cherries, etc.)

Preheat the oven to 350 degrees. Melt the butter in a large baking pan, with sides at least 3 inches high. (A Pyrex dish is fine, or a quart casserole.) Combine the rest of the ingredients except for the fruit and mix together well with a fork. Pour batter into the pan. Slice the fruit into uniform slices, being sure to drain any excess juices from canned fruit so the batter will not be soggy when baked. Arrange the fruit over the top of the batter. (It will sink down somewhat.) Bake for 45 to 50 minutes.

Variations
Combine apples with raisins or currants.
Sprinkle poppy or sesame seeds over the fruit.

Mix walnuts (or pecans) and candied fruit with fresh fruit. Serves 6 to 8.

MINTY PINEAPPLE SLUSH

A very simple and elegant finish to a rich meal. Buy a large can of pineapple chunks packed *in juice* (less cloyingly sweet than the syrup-packed variety) and put the unopened can in the freezer for a few hours. Open the can about 15 minutes before serving, and break the frozen pineapple apart with a fork. Immediately before serving, pour ¼ cup white or green crème de menthe over the slushy pineapple. If you can find them, garnish with fresh mint leaves.

Serves 4.

APRICOT SOUFFLÉ PUDDING

This dessert soufflé is much easier than the tricky French version.

- ½ cup cooked, dried apricots
- 1 cup plus 3 tablespoons sugar
- Grated rind of 1 lemon
- ¼ pound butter or margarine (1 stick), softened
- 5 eggs, separated
- ¼ teaspoon salt

Preheat the oven to 350 degrees. Cook the apricots with 3 tablespoons of the sugar and mash with a fork or purée in a blender. Add the half cup of sugar and the lemon rind and blend well. Mix the softened butter and egg yolks together thoroughly with a fork, adding the yolks one at a time. Stir in the salt. Combine this with the apricot purée and stir thoroughly. Whip the egg whites until they form soft peaks, and very gently fold into the first mixture. Pour carefully into a buttered 1½ quart baking dish (or straight-sided soufflé mold). Bake for 35 minutes and serve hot from the oven.

Serves 4 to 6.

FRUIT COMPOTE

A delicious and very simple dessert, fruit compote is also an excellent side dish with plain roasted meat and fowl. This basic recipe allows you to choose your own favorite dried fruits. It will keep for weeks in the refrigerator.

> 1-pound package mixed dried fruit, or any combination of dried fruits, such as apricots, peaches, pears, prunes, currants, raisins
> Water to cover
> 1 lemon, thinly sliced
> 1 juice orange, thinly sliced
> Honey or sugar to taste

These directions are sketchy, but sufficient. You can start to make the compote the night before by soaking your choice of fruits in warm water. Otherwise, put the fruit into a small saucepan, cover with water, and add thinly sliced lemon and orange. Simmer slowly until the fruits plump up. You may add sugar or honey to taste, but often it is not necessary since the fruits have a natural sweetness. Cool and keep in a covered jar or bowl. For a pleasant contrast in texture, you can also add nut meats—pecans or walnuts—to the mixture after it is cooked.

DRIED FRUIT CHUTNEY

This is not really a chutney, but if you are off somewhere without access to a store that sells the real thing, add ¼ cup vinegar and ½ teaspoon salt to the fruit compote recipe. It will make a respectable substitute for chutney to serve with curry or as a side dish for cold meats.

OLD-FASHIONED BREAD PUDDING

1½ cups soft bread crumbs (stale bread is actually better)
2 cups milk
4 tablespoons butter or margarine, softened
½ cup plus 1 tablespoon sugar
2 eggs, separated
Juice and grated rind of ½ lemon
Pinch of salt

Preheat oven to 325 degrees. Soak the bread crumbs in the milk. Cream the butter and ½ cup of the sugar together, then add the egg yolks, grated rind, and lemon juice. Blend together well with a fork, then stir in the moistened bread crumbs. Bake in a loaf pan about 25 minutes until firm. While the pudding is baking, whip the egg whites with a pinch of salt and 1 tablespoon of sugar until they form high stiff peaks. Carefully pour over the pudding and return to the oven for a few minutes until the meringue is lightly browned. Serve hot or cold.

Variations
Add ¼ cup nutmeats and raisins to the batter.
Add ¼ cup candied fruit bits to the batter.
Serves 6.

CHOCOLATE MOUSSE

Here's a delightfully chocolaty dessert that does not have to be cooked. You'll need a double boiler, or put an asbestos pad under the pot to keep the chocolate squares from burning. (If you are really careful, you can do it very slowly over a conventional flame or heat source.)

8 ounces bittersweet (Baker's) chocolate
1 tablespoon butter
8 eggs, separated
½ cup finely granulated sugar

Combine the chocolate and butter in the top of a double boiler and melt over low heat. (To speed melting, you can shave or grate the chocolate, if you wish.) Beat the egg yolks until light, add the sugar gradually, and continue beating until thoroughly mixed. Add the melted chocolate and butter to the egg and sugar mixture, stirring with a wooden spoon. Beat the egg whites with a wire whisk or electric mixer until they are very stiff and dry, then gently fold into the chocolate mixture until just blended. Pour into a pretty serving bowl, or individual cups, and refrigerate. The mousse will last a couple of days (if you can keep anyone from eating it before that).

Serves 6 to 8.

Variations

Add 2 to 3 tablespoons rum or brandy to the chocolate as it melts.

Whip 1 cup of heavy cream with 4 tablespoons of sugar until stiff, and spoon over each portion when serving, shaving another square of chocolate on the top.

YOGURT CAKE

This interesting and substantial cake is almost foolproof. I have made it in at least a dozen different ways and it turns out beautifully each time. Try it plain, or with any one of the variations. Depending on altitudes and ovens, it may need to bake a bit longer. But don't worry: When a toothpick inserted into the center comes out clean, the cake is done.

½ cup (1 stick) butter or margarine, softened
2 cups granulated sugar; or 1 cup each white and brown sugar
½ teaspoon vanilla
2 eggs
2½ cups flour
½ teaspoon baking soda
Pinch of salt
1 cup yogurt (plain, vanilla, or any other flavor)
Honey (optional)

Preheat the oven to 375 degrees. Cream together the softened butter and sugar until light and fluffy. Add the vanilla and eggs and mix well. Sift together the flour, baking soda, and salt, and add, alternately with the yogurt, to the butter and sugar mixture. Stir with a fork until the batter is thoroughly mixed. Turn the batter into a greased 10- by 14-inch pan, an angel food pan, or a pair of layer cake pans. Bake for 30 to 40 minutes, until a toothpick inserted into the center comes out clean. Cool 10 minutes before removing from the pan. Drizzle honey on top while still warm.

If you prepare it as a layer cake, you can use any frosting or preserves you wish, spreading the filling between the layers and on top. It is delicious and very simple to put together.

Variations

Add 3 tablespoons of cocoa to the batter. You can stir this through the whole batter or try mixing it with only half the batter, then combine the 2 batters and stir together just until you achieve a marbleized effect.

Add 1 tablespoon instant coffee to the batter.
Add ½ cup chopped nuts to the batter.
Add ¼ cup raisins or currants to the batter.

ICE CREAM CAKE

With just a bit of pre-preparation, this dessert can be a showy finish to a simple meal. If you do not wish to make the yogurt cake from scratch, use any firm pound cake from the bakery.

1 recipe yogurt cake (page 208)
1 quart firmly frozen ice cream
½ cup coarsely chopped pecans or walnuts
½ cup Cointreau or dark rum
Aluminum foil

Slice the cake into even ¾-inch-thick slices. Alternate with equal size slices of the ice cream and reassemble into the cake's original shape, pressing the slices together firmly. Top with the nutmeats and wrap in aluminum foil, returning to the freezer until ready for serving. Pour the liquor over the cake just before serving.

Serves 8.

Note: The ice cream can be of your choice, since the cake is equally good with fruit-flavored, chocolate or vanilla. I have used butter pecan and egg nog ice cream, but pick your favorite. You might want to buy a pint each of two different flavors for variety. Be sure that the ice cream is frozen hard before working with it.

ZUPPA INGLESE (TRIFLE)

Supposedly, the Neapolitans called this dessert "English soup" in gratitude for Lord Nelson's victory over Napoleon's fleet in 1798. In any case, it resembles English trifle and is a wonderful mishmash of sweets with a hundred variations. Here is one of them.

- 2 8-inch layer cakes, unfrosted (or an equivalent amount of sponge or pound cake)
- ½ cup rum or sherry
- Strawberry or raspberry preserves
- ¼ cup chopped pecans or walnuts, or slivered almonds
- ¼ cup candied fruit, or raisins and currants
- 1 3- to 4-ounce package instant vanilla pudding, made with milk
- Whipped topping

Start with somewhat stale cake. Cut it into 2- to 3-inch cubes and soak with the rum or sherry. Place about ⅓ of these cubes in the bottom of a deep dish. Spread the preserves on top of the cake, sprinkle with some of the nuts and candied fruit, and ⅓ of the vanilla pudding. Then alternate the remaining ingredients in layers, top with the whipped topping, and garnish with some candied fruit and chopped nuts. It is a great favorite with anyone who has a real sweet tooth.

Serves 6 to 8.

Variations

You can use your own imagination to vary the recipe: Use shaved bittersweet chocolate instead of jam, coffee cake instead of sponge layers, butterscotch pudding instead of vanilla. Enjoy yourself—serve it as the last dessert on a trip and use up all the extra sweets you have on hand!

20

The Language of Cooking:

A Glossary and Conversion Tables

Al dente: Italian for "to the tooth." It means cooked but still firm to the bite, as applied to pasta (spaghetti, macaroni, noodles).

Au gratin: French; a dish browned in the oven or under the broiler, usually covered with grated cheese or buttered bread crumbs.

Au jus: French; meaning served with its natural juices (roast beef is often served this way).

Barbecue: To cook over live coals, usually outdoors, often with repeated applications of a spicy sauce.

Baste: To brush or spoon a sauce or liquid (sometimes butter) over food as it cooks, to add flavor and keep it from drying out. Especially necessary in roasting meats and fowl.

Batter: An uncooked mixture, usually of flour, liquid, and other ingredients, which is thin enough to pour (i.e., cake, crepe, or pancake batter).

Beat: To mix thoroughly with a spoon, fork, whisk, rotary beater, or electric mixer with a vigorous, regular movement.

Buerre: The French word for butter.

Buerre manié: A French term for uncooked butter and flour mixed together into a paste for thickening a sauce.

Buerre noir: French for butter heated to dark brown color.

Buerre noisette: French for butter cooked to the color of amber.

Bisque: A creamy soup, often with shellfish.

Blanch: To immerse in boiling water briefly, to loosen skins (as with almonds or tomatoes), or remove color or strong flavor.

Blend: To mix ingredients together.
Braise: To brown quickly in butter or fat before cooking slowly in a liquid.
Bread: To coat with bread crumbs.
Brown: To cook at a high heat, uncovered, in fat until brown; also can be done in oven or under broiler.
Bruise: To gently crush to release flavor, as with garlic or fresh herbs.
Brulé: French; literally meaning burned, but in cooking it refers to foods glazed with caramelized sugar. French crème caramel is made this way.
Butterfly: To split down the center and open, thus resembling a butterfly. Done with shrimp, fish fillets, small steaks.
Candy: To preserve with or cook in sugar or sugar syrup.
Caramelize: To heat sugar until it melts into a dense brownish syrup.
Chiffonade: French; meaning a garnish of shredded vegetables.
Chop: To cut into small pieces.
Clarify: Literally, to make clear. With liquids, it can be done by adding raw egg whites and heating, then straining through a cloth. With butter, melt gently and strain through cheesecloth. (This is often used in Indian curry recipes, called *Ghee.*)
Clove (of garlic): One individual section of the bulb.
Coat: To cover with a dry or liquid ingredient.
Combine: To mix together.
Coq: The French word for rooster. (Although coq au vin—cock or rooster with wine—may be made with a regular chicken.)
Core: To remove the center, as with apples, pears.
Cream: To mix together until smooth and creamy, as in blending butter and sugar when making a cake.
Crème: French for cream.
Crepes: Thin French pancakes served with a variety of fillings.
Croûte: The French word for crust. En croûte means in a pastry shell or crust.
Crumble: To break into small pieces.

Cure: To preserve foods by salting, smoking, or drying.

Cut in: To blend solid fats into dry mixtures by repeatedly chopping with a knife and fork until coarsely textured and consistent.

Deglaze: To add a liquid to the juices in the cooking pan after removing the main contents, to make a gravy or sauce.

Degrease: To remove the fat from the top of a dish or sauce, either skimming it off while hot or, easier still, cooling it and removing it as a solid.

Devil: To mix finely chopped ingredients, such as eggs or meats, with spicy seasonings (often mustard and pepper sauces), as a filling or spread.

Dice: To cut into fine cubes.

Dilute: To thin by adding liquid, often water or stock, to a dish or sauce.

Disjoint: For fowl, to cut apart at the joint.

Dissolve: To thoroughly mix a solid (sugar, salt, flour) into a liquid.

Dot: To distribute small bits of butter or solid fats on the surface evenly.

Dough: A mixture of flour and other ingredients that is stiff enough to work with the hands.

Drain: To pour off liquids.

Draw: To remove entrails from, or eviscerate, fish or game.

Dredge: To coat lightly with powdered dry ingredients.

Dress: To draw. (Poultry is often called dressed when it is sold cleaned and ready for cooking.)

Drippings: Juices and fat that are released from meat during cooking.

Drizzle: To pour liquids in a fine stream over or into a dish.

Dust: To coat lightly, as with powdered sugar or flour.

En brochette: French; meaning broiled and served on a skewer. Shish kebob is made en brochette.

Entrée: The main course.

Extract: Concentrated flavoring. Vanilla extract is one of the most familiar.

Eviscerate: See *Draw*.

Farce (pronounced, Far-see): French; meaning finely ground meat or fish, combined with other ingredients as a stuffing or filling.

Fillet (or Filet): Boneless meat or fish. Filet mignon is beef tenderloin.

Filter: To remove particles by straining through a porous material.

Flake: To break into small thin pieces with a fork. (Tuna is available as flakes.)

Flambé: French; meaning served with flaming liquids; usually refers to desserts with flavored brandies or liqueurs lighted at the last moment to burn off the alcohol.

Florentine: Prepared with spinach and usually covered with a cheese sauce.

Fold: To gently incorporate into a mixture without breaking down whipped ingredients. Aerated ingredients like whipped cream or egg whites are folded into batters to keep their lightness when combined with heavier ingredients.

French fry: To fry in deep fat.

Fricassee: Poultry or meat simmered in a creamy sauce, sometimes with vegetables.

Fromage: The French word for cheese.

Frost: To glaze with a coating of crystallized sugar, or to cover with a solid sugar, butter mixture—to frost a cake.

Fry: To cook with fat in a pan or skillet.

Garnish: To decorate foods before serving, using parsley, cherries, etc.

Gel: To congeal, sometimes by the addition of gelatin or pectin.

Gâteau: The French word for cake.

Giblets: The liver, heart, and kidneys of fowl.

Glace: The French word for ice cream.

Glacé: French; meaning sugared or candied, usually fruits.

Glaze: To cover with a sauce or liquid to make foods shiny.

Grate: To shave foods into very small particles.

Gratinée: The French word for a crust of cheese or buttered crumbs over a casserole or other dish.

Grease: To rub with butter or fat.

Grill: Either the device used to keep foods over a charcoal fire or the act of cooking in this manner.

Grind: To mill into fine particles with a grinder.

Hull, Husk: To remove the outer covering, as from nuts, corn.

Ice: To apply frosting, or to chill.

Infusion: A liquid, usually hot, in which ingredients have been steeped to extract flavor. The French call herbal teas infusions.

Jell: See *Gel.*

Julienne: French; meaning cut into small strips, like matchsticks.

Knead: To work with the hands into a smooth mixture. Used for combining ingredients that are too thick to stir.

Lait: The French word for milk.

Lard: To insert bits of lard or other solid fat into meats to keep them moist while cooking.

Leaven: To make doughs and batters rise with the addition of yeast, baking powder, or baking soda.

Line: To cover the inner surface of a cooking vessel with a food (for instance, crumbs) or other material (paper, foil) before adding the main ingredients.

Marinate: To soak in a flavored liquid before cooking. The liquid is called the marinade.

Marrow: The tissue filling the cavity of a bone, considered a delicacy.

Mash: To reduce to a pulp.

Meat glaze: A rich brown sauce made by cooking a meat stock until it is concentrated.

Medallion: In French, the small center cut of choice meat, usually beef, often covered in a rich sauce when served.

Mince: To chop or cut into extremely fine pieces.

Mocha: A mixture of coffee and chocolate.

Mold: To chill or freeze in a shaped container; also, the container itself.

THE LANGUAGE OF COOKING 217

Mortar and pestle: A strong bowl with a heavy crushing implement for pulverizing and blending foods in small quantities; especially useful for crushing herbs and spices.

Mull: To heat, sweeten, and spice wine, ale, or fruit juices.

Noisette: The French word for hazelnut; or a small nut-shaped piece of meat, usually lamb.

Oeuf: The French word for egg.

Pain: The French word for bread.

Pan-fry: See *Sauté*.

Pare: To remove the peel of vegetables, fruits, with a knife or other tool.

Paste: A smooth blend of materials.

Pâté: Ground or minced foods.

Peel: To remove the skin or outer layer.

Pepper: To add pepper, or coat with ground pepper.

Pickle: To preserve in vinegar or brine.

Pinch: Less than ⅛ teaspoon; just a sprinkle.

Plank: To broil and serve meats on a wooden plank.

Pluck; To remove feathers from a fowl.

Plump: To fill out dehydrated foods (raisins, for instance) by soaking in a liquid.

Poach: To simmer slowly in a liquid.

Poisson: The French word for fish.

Poulet: The French word for chicken.

Pound: To flatten with a mallet or other heavy instrument.

Prick: To make small punctures in the skin or crust of foods to allow trapped steam or juices to escape. Usually done with a fork.

Purée: To mill, pound, grind, or sieve into a paste.

Ragout: A hearty stew.

Reconstitute: To add liquids to dehydrated foods to restore their natural moist state.

Reduce: To boil away extra liquids in order to concentrate flavors.

Render: To cook away fat from meat, which is then usually drained off.

Rice: To put soft foods through a finely perforated implement called a ricer to create a consistency resembling that of rice. Usually used with cooked potatoes.

Roast: To cook in an oven with dry heat.

Roe: Fish eggs (caviar).

Roux: A cooked butter and flour mixture, often with spices, used for thickening sauces.

Sambal: Side dish of condiments served with curries.

Sauté: To fry quickly on top of the stove, or in an open fry pan, with a little fat.

Scald: To heat almost to the point of boiling.

Scallop: To bake in a cream sauce, covered with buttered bread crumbs.

Score: To make shallow slices with a sharp knife, often to hasten cooking and rendering of fats.

Scrape: To remove a thin skin, as that of a vegetable, by pushing a sharp blade across the surface.

Sear: To brown meats quickly, usually on top of the stove, to keep juices sealed within.

Season: To enhance the flavor of food by adding salt, herbs, spices, or other condiments; also, to build up a protective coating on cast-iron cooking pans.

Shell: To remove an outer covering, such as a pod, shell, or husk (as from nuts, shellfish, peas, corn).

Shirr: To bake eggs with cream and sometimes other ingredients in a shallow heatproof dish.

Shred: To cut food into thin strips (cole slaw, for instance).

Shuck: See *Shell*.

Sieve: To strain; also, the strainer itself.

Sift: To pass flour and other dry ingredients through a strainer or sifter.

Simmer: To cook over low heat (approximately 185 degrees) until a few bubbles appear on the surface.

Singe: To burn off hairs or feathers over an open flame.

Skewer: To pass foods and meats in uniform-size pieces onto a metal or wooden pin; also, the pin itself. See also *En brochette*.

Skim: To remove fat or other material that rises to the surface of cooking liquids with spoon or syringe.

Sliver: To cut or slice into fine, thin pieces, as almonds or chocolate.

Soak: To let stand in liquid.

Steam: To cook, covered, over small amounts of water or boiling liquids without actually immersing the food in the liquid. A valuable way to retain vitamins in vegetables.

Steep: To let dry ingredients (tea, for example) remain in a liquid to release flavors. See *Infusion.*

Stew: To cook slowly, submerged in liquid.

Stir: To mix, usually with a circular motion.

Stir-fry: The Oriental method of quickly cooking small uniformly cut pieces of food, turning them often as they fry.

Stock: The strained broth or liquid from cooked meats, poultry, fish, or vegetables; used as soup or as the base for sauces.

Strain: To separate liquids from solids in a sieve, strainer, or colander.

Stud: To insert pieces (cloves, garlic) into the surface of food.

Terrine: The French word for an earthenware container used for baking pâtés or other ground meats. Also, the foods made in a terrine.

Timbale: An individual mold of meat or vegetables, often thickened in a custard sauce.

Toss: To mix thoroughly with a turning motion; for example, salad.

Truss: To tie up, as with the wings and legs of poultry, to make more compact for cooking. Use cotton thread or string.

Vin: The French word for wine.

Volaille: The French word for poultry.

Whip: To beat into a froth with an electric or rotary beater, whisk, or fork. A blender will *not* whip cream or eggs.

Wok: An Oriental bowl-shaped cooking pot with a round bottom for preparing stir-fried and many other Chinese and Japanese foods.

Table of Weights and Measures

Pinch or dash = less than 1/8 teaspoon
3 teaspoons = 1 tablespoon
2 tablespoons = 1 fluid ounce
1 jigger = 1½ fluid ounces
4 tablespoons = ¼ cup
8 tablespoons = ½ cup
16 tablespoons = 1 cup
1 cup = 8 fluid ounces
2 cups = 1 pint
1 pint = 16 fluid ounces
2 pints = 1 quart
1 quart = 32 fluid ounces
4 quarts = 1 gallon
1 gallon = 64 fluid ounces
1 ounce = 1/16 pound
2 ounces = 1/8 pound
4 ounces = ¼ pound
8 ounces = ½ pound
16 ounces = 1 pound

Miscellaneous

1 stick of butter = ¼ pound = 4 ounces
    = ½ cup = 8 tablespoons
1 cup grated or finely shredded cheese = approximately ¼ pound

Metric Equivalents for Liquid Ingredients

1 fluid ounce = 29.6 milliliters
4 fluid ounces = 118.3 milliliters
8 fluid ounces (1 cup) = 236.6 milliliters (.24 liters)
1 pint (2 cups) = .473 liters
1 quart (2 pints) = .946 liters
1 gallon (4 quarts) = 3.785 liters

Metric Equivalents for Dry Ingredients

1 ounce = 28.35 grams
4 ounces = 113.4 grams
8 ounces = 226.8 grams
1 pound = 453.6 grams (.454 kilograms)

Oven Temperatures (Fahrenheit)

Warm = 200 degrees
Very slow = below 300 degrees
Slow = 300 degrees
Moderate = 350 degrees
Hot = 400 degrees
Very hot = 450 degrees
Broil = 500 degrees and hotter (open flame or electric coil)

Fahrenheit/Centigrade (Celsius) Conversion Scale

0 degrees centigrade (Celsius) = 32 degrees Fahrenheit
= freezing point of water
100 degrees centigrade (Celsius) = 212 degrees Fahrenheit
= boiling point of water

To convert centigrade (Celsius) to Fahrenheit:

> Multiply the centigrade degrees by 9, then divide by 5 and add 32.

To convert Fahrenheit to centigrade (Celsius):

> Subtract 32 from the Fahrenheit degrees, multiply by 5, and then divide by 9.

Recipe Index

Antipasto, 89
Apricot soufflé pudding, 205
Asparagus, 196
    and chicken mornay, 162
    curried, omelet with cheese, 123
    and ham vinaigrette, 172
    vinaigrette, 196–197
Avgolemono, 103
Avocado, guacamole, 114

Bacon omelet, 123
Bean soup, black, 99
Beans, "crumby" green, 197
Beef
    barbecuing, 129–130
    braised, en daube, 150–151
    carbonnades à la flamande, 147–148
    chopped, with anchovies, 144
    hamburgers, 130, 142–144
    meat loaf, Marshall's, 145–146
    pepper steak
        Chinese, 137
        French, 135–136
    roast, classic, 132–133
    steak
        au poivre, 135–136
        tartare, 96, 134–135
    stew
        French, à la Marseilles, 146–147
        Russian, with cabbage, 148–150
    Stroganoff, 138
    in wine and mustard sauce, 151–152
Black bean soup, 99
Bouillon, 100
Bouquet garni, 67
Bread
    garlic, 152
    stuffed French, 89–90

Caesar salad, 110–111
Cake
    ice cream, 209–210
    yogurt, 208–209
Carrots, with dill, 197
Cauliflower, with brown butter, 198

224 RECIPE INDEX

Caviar, 96
  omelet, 124
Champagne, 25, 171–172
Cheese
  grilled, and liver pâté hors d'oeuvres, 97
  serving, 26
Cherry soup, cold Hungarian, 107–108
Chicken, 156–170
  amontillado, 158–159
  and asparagus, mornay, 162
  barbecuing, 130
  breasts
    Orientale, 167–168
    with pistachio nuts, 169
  Byzantine, 166–167
  curried, with zucchini, 165–166
  livers
    and bacon in wine sauce, 170
    chopped, 91–92
  with oregano, 160
  paprika, 164–165
  in the pot, 160–161
  roast, 156–157
Chili, 139–141
  casserole, 141
  cubed steak, 141
  and eggs, 141
  Mexicana, 141
  and rice, 141
Chinese
  egg drop soup, 52
  fried rice, 194–195
  pepper steak, 137
Chocolate mousse, 207–208

Choucroute, 171–172
Chutney, dried fruit, 206
Clam chowder, Cape Cod, 107
Coffee
  as flavoring, 37
  hobo, 37
Cole slaw, 114–115
Coq au vin, 162–163
Court bouillon, 179
Cranberry sauce, 87
Cream cheese
  and chutney, 90
  fillings for hors d'oeuvres, 95–96
Crepes, 125–126
Crudités, 24, 93
Curried chicken with zucchini, 165–166
Curried seafood, 185–186
Curry powder, 68

Desserts, 125, 204–211
  apricot soufflé pudding, 205
  bread pudding, 207
  chocolate mousse, 207–208
  fruit
    cobbler, 204–205
    compote, 206
  ice cream cake, 209–210
  minty pineapple slush, 205
  omelets, 125
  trifle, 210–211
  yogurt cake, 208–209
  zuppa inglese, 210–211
Deviled
  eggs, 118–119
    in aspic, 119–120
  sardines, 96

Egg drop soup, 52
Eggs, 117–125
  Benedict, 120
  boiled, *see* Hard- and soft-cooked
  cooked
    hard, 117–118
    soft, 117–118
  deviled, 118–119
    in aspic, 119–120
  Florentine, 121
  fried, 118
  omelets, 121–125
    asparagus and cheese, curried, 123
    bacon, 123
    basic, 122
    caviar, 124
    dessert, 125
    herb, 124
    from leftovers, 124
    mushroom, 123
    spinach and cheese, 122
    tomato, 123
  poached, 118
Egg salad, curried with tuna, 90, 116

Fettuccine Alfredo, 189
Fines herbes, 69
Fish, 91, 175–187
  baked, 179–180
  barbecuing, 130
  broiled
    charcoal, 177
    oven, 177
  fried, 180
  poached, 178
  roasted in foil, 130
  salmon croquettes, 183
  sautéed, 176–177
    Theodora, 181–182
  sesame roulades, 180–181
  See also shellfish
Fruit
  cobbler, 204–205
  compote, 206

Garlic
  bread, 152
  marinade, 86
  mayonnaise, 79
Gravy, pan, 84
Guacamole, 114

Hamburgers, 130, 142–144
Herb
  mayonnaise, 79
  omelet, 124
Herbes de Provence, 69–70
Horseradish
  cream sauce, 80
  mayonnaise, 81

Ice cream cake, 209–210

Jewish chicken soup, 104

Kasha, 195
  varnishkes, 195
Kebobs, 129, 130

226 RECIPE INDEX

Lamb
  barbecuing, 130
Lasagna, 190–191
Leftovers
  for Chinese fried rice, 194–195
  in omelets, 124
  trifle, 210–211
Lemon
  and butter sauce, 84
  marinade, 86
  with ravioli, 191–192
Lox, 91

Marinades, 84–87
  cooked wine marinade for game, 87
  garlic, 86
  lemon, 86
  oriental, 85–86
Matzo
  balls, 105
  brei, 128
Mayonnaise
  basic blender, 78–79
  curried, 79
  garlic, 79
  herb, 79
  horseradish, 81
  watercress, 79–80
Mousse, chocolate, 207–208
Mushrooms
  pickled (*Champignons à la Grecque*), 88
  sautéed, 200
  stuffed, 199–200

Niçoise, salade, 109–110

Omelets, *see* Eggs
Onion soup, French, gratinée, 100–101
Oriental sauce, 85–86

Pasta
  fettuccine Alfredo, 189
  lasagna, 190–191
  ravioli with lemon and butter, 191–192
  with white clam sauce, 188
Pastry shells, filled, 98
Pâté, chicken liver, 91–92
  with grilled cheese, 97
Pineapple slush, minty, 205
Pissaladière, 96–97
Pork, 130, 172–174
  barbecuing, 130
  chops, oriental style, 172–173
  Montmorency, 173–174
Pudding
  apricot soufflé, 205
  old-fashioned bread, 207
  Yorkshire, 133–134

Quiches, 126
  crabmeat, 127
  Lorraine, 127
  onion, 127

Ratatouille, 90, 200–201
Ravioli, with lemon and butter, 191–192
Rice, Chinese fried, 194–195

Salad dressings
  classic French vinaigrette, 76–77
  Russian, 80
  sour cream blue cheese, 77
  Thousand Island, 80
  See also Sauces
Salads, 24, 109–116
  Caesar, 110–111
  cole slaw, 114–115
  crudités, 24, 93
  cucumber and yogurt, 115
  "farmer's chop suey," 115
  guacamole, 114
  Niçoise, 109–110
  spinach and mushroom, 112
    wilted spinach, 113
  tarama, 113–114
  tuna and egg, curried, 90, 116
  vegetable, with sour cream, 115
  "wilderness," 38
Salmon
  croquettes, 183
  smoked, 91
Sauces, 72–87
  Béchamel, 81–82
  brown, 83
  cranberry, 87
  horseradish cream, 80
  lemon butter, 84
  mayonnaise
    basic blender, 78–79
    curried, 79
    garlic, 79
    herbed, 79
    horseradish, 81
    watercress, 79–80
  mayonnaise-based
    mock Hollandaise, 81
    Russian dressing, 80
    tartar, 80
    Thousand Island, 80
  mornay, 82
  oriental, 85–86
  pesto, 193
  rémoulade, 84
  soubise, 82
  tomato, classic Italian, 192–193
  velouté
    basic, 82–83
    tarragon, 83
  white
    basic, 81–82
    clam, 188
    super-rich, 83
Schnitzel à la Holstein, 154
Shellfish, 92, 184–187
  baked, 179–180
  broiled
    charcoal, 177
    oven, 177
  curried, 185–186
  de Jonghe, 184–185
  pasta with white clam sauce, 188
  poached, 178
  sautéed, 176–177
  scampi, 184
  Szechuan, 186–187
  See also Fish
Shrimp with dill, 92
Soups, 52, 99–108

RECIPE INDEX

avgolemono, 103
black bean, 99
bouillon, 100
cherry, cold Hungarian, 107–108
chicken, Jewish, 104
clam chowder, Cape Cod, 107
egg drop, Chinese, 52
gazpacho, 101–102
matzo ball, 104–105
onion, French, gratinée, 100–101
spinach, cold, 105–106
Stock, 100
  beef, 100
  chicken, 100
  frozen cubes, 100
Stracciatella alla Romana, 102–103
Vegetable, with leftovers, 99
Squash
  acorn, 202
  zucchini, oriental style, 203
Spinach
  and cheese omelet, 122
  Italian style, 201–202
  mimosa, 52
  and mushroom salad, 112
  salad, wilted, 113
  soup, cold, 105–106
Steak
  au poivre, French, 135–136
  pepper
    Chinese, 137
    French, 135–136
  tartare, 96, 134–135

Stews
  beef à la Marseilles, French, 146–147
  beef and cabbage, Russian, 148–150
  beef in wine and mustard sauce, 151–152
  carbonnades à la Flamande, 147–148
  chicken in the pot, 160–161
  ratatouille, 90, 200–201
Stracciatella alla Romana, 102
Stuffed
  French bread, 89–90
  mushrooms, 199–200
  raw vegetables, 94–95
Stuffing, poultry, 157–158

Tarama salad, 113–114
Tomato omelet, 123
  sauce, classic Italian, 192–193
Trifle, 210-211
Tuna salad, curried egg and, 116

Veal, 153–155
  breaded cutlets, 153–154
  with Marsala, 155
  piccata, 154–155
  schnitzel à la Holstein, 154
Vegetables, 196–203
  asparagus vinaigrette, 196–197
  beans, "crumby" green, 197
  carrots with dill, 197

cauliflower with brown butter, 198
endive, braised, 198–199
mushrooms
    sautéed, 200
    stuffed, 199–200
ratatouille, 200–201
roast in foil, 130–131
spinach
    Italian style, 201–202
    mimosa, 52
zucchini, oriental style, 202–203
Vinaigrette dressing, Classic French, 76–77
Vinegar, flavored, 55–56
Vodka, flavored, 55–56

Watercress mayonnaise, 79–80
White sauce (Béchamel), 81–82
    super-rich, 83

Yogurt cake, 208–209
Yorkshire pudding, 133–134

Zucchini, oriental style, 202–203
zuppa inglese, 210–211